Mental Health and Illness

Questions and Answers for Counsellors and Therapists

Mental Health and Illness

Questions and Answers for Counsellors and Therapists

By

DAWN FRESHWATER

Bournemouth University

with contributions from
JENI BOYD and SABI REDWOOD

Series Editor
MICHAEL JACOBS

W
WHURR PUBLISHERS

060081260

Contents

About the author

Dawn Freshwater is currently Professor of Mental Health, Institute of Health and Community Studies, Bournemouth University. She is a United Kingdom Council for Psychotherapy (UKCP) registered psychotherapist and an experienced supervisor and trainer. She has authored, co-authored and edited several books and numerous papers, and is editor of *Journal of Psychiatric and Mental Health Nursing*.

Contributors

Jeni Boyd has completed a Masters degree in Jungian Studies at the University of Essex Centre for Psychoanalyic Studies. Her major dissertation was on 'the shamanic potential of the individual' and her recent Research Masters in Counselling and Psychotherapy at Nottingham Trent University focused on the liminal space of the dream-world. Her interest in dream-work and in the interface between differing ideologies is being further explored through a PhD at The University of Manchester. Her past experiences as a user of Secondary Mental Health services underpin and inform her present work as a counsellor in Primary Care.

Sabi Redwood is employed as Senior Lecturer in Research at the Institute of Health and Community Studies at Bournemouth University, leading the undergraduate and postgraduate critical appraisal and research curricula at the school. Her background is in child health nursing and clinical leadership. She is involved in a number of projects concerned with ethics, difference and diversity and their role in the education of health care professionals. In addition, she has been a Mental Health Service user for many years.

CHAPTER 1

An introduction to mental health and mental illness

Mental health concerns everyone. It affects our ability to cope with and manage change, life events and transitions such as bereavement or retirement. All human beings have mental health needs, no matter what the state of their psyche. Mental health needs can be met in a variety of settings including acute hospital settings, primary care settings, self-help groups, through social services and of course through counselling and psychotherapy. This book is written specifically for counsellors and psychotherapists, working from any theoretical orientation and across the public and private sector, with a view to providing guidance on working with individuals who are experiencing mental illness. The background to the current context of mental health care, treatment and management both within the United Kingdom and internationally is outlined. Ways of defining mental health are discussed as a means of drawing attention to the complex and diverse understanding of what constitutes mental illness. This chapter also provides a general overview of the book along with some broad guidelines about how to make the most of the text. Relevant local and national policies are referred to in order to bring the reader's attention to the contemporary changes in mental health care as they impact on the work of the counsellor and psychotherapist.

Defining mental health and illness

Psychological distress is to some extent necessary for people to function; without the heightened awareness and sensitivity that psychological distress brings to social situations and life experiences we may find ourselves risking our lives at one extreme and under performing at the other. However, there is a point at which psychological distress can topple over into what might be termed or diagnosed as a mental disorder. At what point health promoting and seemingly 'normal' responses can be defined and classified as mental illness is, as one might expect, debatable and highly contentious. Mental health and mental illness can be thought of as a continuum, rather than a polarised dichotomy, with people positioned at various points depending on life events (external factors), genetic inheritance and stages of development (internal factors). There are many definitions of mental health, the majority of which are simplistic, partial and inevitably subjective. To locate and subscribe to one definition not only reinforces the belief that the concept of mental health can be pinpointed and concretised, but of course it is in itself also too simplistic and partial. Indeed those appointed to draft the *Diagnostic and Statistical Manual of Mental Disorders* (DMS-IV) (American Psychiatric Association, 1994) themselves argued that the term mental disorder could not be a more unfortunate term, preserving as it does an outdated mind–body duality (Kendall, 1996). (See Chapter 2, question 2.1 for a comprehensive explanation of the DSM-IV). Tudor (2004) argues that it is more helpful to think in terms of concepts of mental health and illness. This idea was first adopted by Jahoda (1958) who identified categories within which concepts of mental health could be represented. He described these as follows:

- mental health is indicated by the attitudes of the individual towards themselves
- mental health is expressed in the individual's style and degree of growth, development or self-actualisation
- mental health is based on the individual's relation to reality in terms of autonomy, perception of reality, environmental mastery
- mental health is the ability of the individual to integrate developing and differing aspects of themselves over time.

Having ascertained that mental illness is not a neutral, value-free, scientifically precise term and as such cannot be clearly defined, we turn now to the issue of normal and abnormal, or, as most commonly referred to, the sane and the insane. It is not easy to distinguish the normal from the abnormal, indeed there is a great deal of conflicting evidence relating to the use of such terms as 'sanity, insanity, mental illness and schizophrenia' (Rosenhan, 2001). Moreover, it is open to question as to whether the diagnoses of mental illness reside in the patients themselves or in the environment. Rosenhan says: 'We might like to believe that we can tell the normal from the abnormal, but the evidence is not compelling...there is a great deal of conflicting data on the reliability, utility and meaning of such terms as "sanity", "insanity", "mental illness", and "schizophrenia"' (2001, p. 70). He goes on to ask: 'Do the salient characteristics that lead to diagnoses reside in the patients themselves or in the environment and contexts in which the observers find them?' Despite these important questions, it is of course necessary to have some way of monitoring the extent to which an individual's behaviour deviates from what is viewed as 'the norm', in order to ascertain a framework for structuring treatment and care. To this end a number of indices have been developed classifying mental health diagnoses. Two of the main classification systems are mentioned below and are referred to throughout the remaining chapters.

Classifying mental illness

Manning (2001, p. 77) argues that the process of classification is 'fundamental to any science'. The two main classification systems used within mental health care are the International Classification of Diseases (ICD-10) developed by the World Health Organization (WHO, 1992) and the Diagnostic and Statistical Manual for Mental Disorders (DSM-IV) (American Psychiatric Association, 1994) (discussed in detail in Chapter 2). Different epochs foster distinct types of mental disorder in its members. The mental disorders that characterise individuals living in contemporary society have implications for all health practitioners including counsellors and psychotherapists. Psychiatrists have for many years distinguished between the major mental illnesses, known as the psychoses (such as schizophrenia) and the neuroses (such as anxiety disorders and phobias). Many counsellors and psychotherapists are already familiar with these terms; however, it is perhaps worth outlining the contemporary thinking around these and other diagnostic categories.

Psychoses are diseases in which the individual's capacity to recognise reality and their ability to make appropriate communications and judgements are seriously impaired. They are sometimes accompanied by the presence of delusions and hallucinations (Craig, 2000). Psychoses can be further divided into functional and organic: the former are associated with a primary disturbance of mood, normally accompanied with some psychotic symptoms (for example schizophrenia); the latter refers to brain pathology that results in psychotic symptoms (as in dementia).

Many psychological theorists have written on the subject of neuroses: Freud (1914) originally wrote of neuroses as repressed conflicts between ego instincts and sexual libido, whereas Jung saw neuroses as being closely related to the individuation process. Jacoby (1990, p. 97) states that 'They often have an ultimate prospective purpose, since their function is to coerce the individual into a new attitude that will further the maturation of his personality'. Whereas Horney (1991) defines neurosis as a disturbance in one's relation to self and to others, neurotics can really only be differentiated from the general population by the degree to which they experience disabling symptoms. Thus, it could be said that where the psychotic person has an uncertain grasp on reality, the neurotic experiences a heightened and debilitating level of stress resulting in such disorders as, for example, obsessive compulsive disorder (OCD) and phobias.

In the recent past one specific psychiatric diagnosis, that of personality disorder, has received a great deal of professional and media attention. One of the most contentious diagnoses, personality disorder is generally defined as consisting of deeply ingrained, enduring behaviours leading the person to behave in socially unacceptable ways. Manning (2001, p. 76) contests that 'personality disorder is the site of considerable psychiatric controversy', stating that it has been 'separated in British legislation from the two conventional conditions of mental illness and mental disability, as a third type of mental disorder – psychopathy'. Sometimes referred to as moral insanity (and occasionally interpreted as borderline), it is the behaviour of such individuals that separates them from the more easily identifiable disturbed mental processes and obvious organic malfunctioning diagnosed in the mentally ill or mentally disabled. In psychoanalytic terms individuals with a personality disorder experience an instability of identity leading to a mixture of alienation from others, feelings of grandiosity, dependency and disdain. There is a tendency to polarise people and project out primitive emotions of rage and shame. Personality disorders can be further classified into sub-groups, three of the most common being anti-social personality disorder (ASPD), paranoid personality disorder (PPD) and emotionally unstable personality disorder (most often associated with 'borderline personality'). There are few treatments that are known to be successful in the management of personality disorders. Where treatment is successful it is heavily reliant on the individual's willingness to accept responsibility for their actions, which in turn requires a degree of introspection and honesty.

It is worth mentioning that classifications of mental disorder also draw distinctions between common mental health problems and serious mental illness (SMI). Unfortunately, attempts to distinguish common mental health problems from serious mental illness have relied heavily on such markers as the presence of a psychotic diagnosis, which as Ryrie and Norman (2004, p. 22) point out, means that 'SMI is synonymous with "psychoses" and common mental health problems with "neuroses"'.

There is a further mode of understanding and organising mental illness, one that is very familiar to most counsellors and psychotherapists, and is linked to psychological schools of thinking such as psychoanalytic and humanistic theories. Psychological frameworks have proved useful in helping to determine treatment plans, and also enable the therapist and client to create a shared understanding of how the client's life processes are unfolding.

Frameworks for understanding mental illness

A number of psychological frameworks have been influential in informing the theory and practice of mental health, and whilst they propose distinct explanations for the aetiology of mental illness and in turn imply different treatment modalities, they also overlap. Those most often referred to are the psychodynamic, behavioural, biological and medical, humanistic and systemic (Dallos, 1996). As previously noted, counsellors and psychotherapists are already well acquainted with these psychological frameworks, and have often been trained as practitioners in at least one of the above modalities. Nevertheless, for the purpose of this book, it might be helpful to revisit each theoretical orientation and outline the way in which mental illness is understood in each.

Biological and medical frameworks (sometimes referred to as the disease model) view psychological problems as resulting, in the main, from physical causes such as brain defects, hereditary factors or as the results of accidents or injury. Recent developments in this area suggest that disorders such as schizophrenia are linked to deficits in neurotransmitters located in the brain and can be inherited through genetic make-up. Further, diseases such as depression are attributed to changes in serotonin levels in the brain or a similar chemical imbalance. The biological model draws on traditional medicine and attempts to identify the presence of a 'stable' phenomenon called mental illness through scientific objectivity. One of the consequences of viewing mental illness in this manner is the belief that such illnesses can be identified and classified (as in the *Diagnostic and Statistical Manual for Mental Disorders* (American Psychiatric Association, 1994) and the International Classification of Disease (World Health Organization, 1992)) (see Question 2.1). Additionally, where a physical or biological cause is identified as the basis of a mental disorder, treatments are in the main determined by a person's biology, leading to the administration of psychotropic drugs, alongside psycho-education and electroconvulsive therapy (Dallos, 1996). There is little doubt that a complex and dynamic interplay exists between the psychological and physical dimensions of the self, and it is well known that many physical diseases can cause or precipitate mental illness, and vice versa (Martin, 1997). In the words of Frances, First and Widiger (1991) 'There is much that is physical in the so-called mental disorders and much mental in the so- called physical disorders. Moreover, writers such as Kendell (1996) point out that: 'The distinction between neurological disorders of the brain like Parkinson's disease and psychiatric disorders like schizophrenia is particularly artificial and can only be understood in the light of the different historical origins of psychiatry and neurology and the unfortunate nineteenth century dichotomy between the mind and brain' (p. 23). This is the focus of the questions in Chapter 3, which clearly defines the relationship between the mind and the body, articulating what effect the physical systems can have on the mind and vice versa. The psyche–soma connection has been long debated and continues to be developed and examined. However, biological frameworks have a tendency to apply and are criticised for applying knowledge in an authoritative way that encourages recipients of treatment to remain passive and submissive. Other frameworks lean towards enabling the individual to learn for and about themselves, although some are more rigid than others.

Behavioural frameworks are closely aligned to learning theories and have long been associated with early exponents of conditioning theories. Symptoms of mental distress, considered to be learned habits, arise from the interaction between external stressors and the individual's personality. Thus, in behavioural models, the symptoms and their associated behaviours are the result of maladaptive responses and as such *are* the mental illness. A diversity of techniques have been developed using behavioural principles including behaviour modification, systematic desensitisation and more latterly cognitive–behavioural (CBT) approaches. Interestingly, although CBT is the youngest psychological model of the ones outlined here, it has become extremely popular since the mid-1990s, and is the preferred choice of counselling intervention in many primary health care settings. Much comparative research has been conducted in the efficacy of this and other psychological treatments, some of which is reviewed in questions in Chapters 6 and 7.

The psychodynamic framework argues that mental health problems are determined by the history of the individual's prior emotional experiences, which unconsciously serve to disrupt the normal path of development through psychosexual or psychosocial stages. Psychodynamic theories can also be seen to draw on a broad range of foundations, including biological and evolutionary theory, religion and the arts and as such 'psychiatric disorders are not viewed as illnesses with disease based causality but as conflicts between different levels of mental functioning' (Ryrie & Norman, 2004, p. 6). Psychodynamic approaches generally view mental health problems as rooted in negative childhood experiences, with treatment emphasising the therapeutic alliance and the effects of early attachments on current relationships.

Whilst humanistic frameworks do not deny the existence of the unconscious, they tend to view the individual as motivated by the need to grow and develop and as potentially creative. Using a holistic approach, humanistic theories are concerned with the integration of all aspects of the person, including dreams, sensations, emotions, cognitions and behaviour.

Systemic frameworks do not locate problems that are residing simply within the individual, but are concerned with the way in which the wider network of relationships influences the patterns and actions of the person. This type of framework is closely related to the social model, in that family beliefs are understood to be related to wider sociological context including shared values and norms. Questions in Chapter 5, with its focus on spiritual aspects of mental illness, highlight some of the ways in which both the social model and systemic models can enhance, delay or prevent treatment. Indeed, Chapter 5 might seem a rather surprising inclusion in this volume, but spiritual beliefs are an important part of many people's lives. Interestingly, many patients with mental health problems have experienced rejection from their place of spiritual worship at the time when they have most needed to feel the unconditional love and kinship of their spiritual community.

The social model, which is referred to in depth in Chapter 4, is predominantly concerned with the way in which people react to unexpected and unpleasant life events. Proponents of the social model are particularly vociferous when it comes to the relationship between the different experiences of some ethnic groups in mental health services, particularly those of the African-Caribbean community. As is pointed out in questions in Chapter 4, persons of African-Caribbean race are more likely to be detained under the mental health act and to be labelled as schizophrenic (Goater, King & Cole 1999). The social model does not have a fixed idea of what constitutes a mental illness; rather psychiatric illness is understood from within the individual's context and cultural society. Sponsors of the social model focus on enabling people to take up an acceptable role in society rather than emphasising corrective behavioural and medical treatments.

Managing mental illness

At least one in four people are affected by a mental health problem at some point in their lives, many of them (about 20 per cent) presenting in primary care settings (Singleton et al., 2001). The *National Service Framework for Mental Health* (Department of Health, 1999a) reports that the incidence of mental illness rises in certain contexts. Influencing factors were mentioned at the beginning of this chapter and include stress, drug and alcohol abuse, social exclusion, traumatic early life experiences and unemployment. (Here incidence is referring to the number of new cases of a disorder that arises within a population, within a given time period, whilst prevalence refers to the number of people with a specific disorder within a given population.) Whilst neurotic problems are the most common form of mental illness (1 in 6), serious mental illness affects approximately 1–2 people in every 100.

The problem of how to manage the mental health of the population is a very real one. By 2020 the World Health Organization (WHO) warns that death from mental health disorders will be the second most common cause of mortality. Reasons for the increase in mental illness abound but remain speculative. Some conclusions about the nature of contemporary mental illness have been made (Freshwater, 2003). Tod Sloan (1996) determines that contentedness seems to be scarce, arguing along with Mirowsky (1989) that this is a price we pay for the lifestyle we call modern. Most people experience some degree of emotional dissonance, ranging from vague anxiety, inability to concentrate, manic work habits, the desire to drug oneself, alienation, estrangement and fantasises of a radical change of lifestyle.

Policy and research developments

As a result of fairly radical and heavily contested changes in mental health policy many people with a severe and/or chronic mental health disorder now live and are cared for in the community. This is usually associated with financial hardship, poor social relationships, lack of employment and a lower than average standard of living. As a result of the recent modernisation agenda, complex mental health services are now delivered by multiple agencies across a varied terrain of disciplines. In 1992 the British Government published its vision for the future and its legislation in the policy document *The Health of the Nation* (Department of Health, 1992). This was followed, and to a certain extent backed up by the subsequent policy document *Our Healthier Nation* (Department of Health, 1999b). Both documents cast cursory glances at the problem of mental illness, which alongside coronary heart disease, cancer and strokes became national targets for health improvement. Since then further focused policy has been developed, most notably the *National Service Framework for Mental Health* (Department of Health, 1999a) and *Making it Happen* (Department of Health, 2001). The *National Service Framework* sets out the agenda for improving mental health services through constituting national standards and increasing investment in mental health services. Such roles as the graduate mental health worker and the gateway worker, early intervention and crisis resolution teams are part of that investment and are the topic of several questions throughout the book.

The new Mental Health Bill (a reform of the 1983 Mental Health Act) is a further development of the overall modernisation of mental health care. Whilst the majority of individuals with mental health problems are not treated under the Mental Health Act, compulsory detention is sometimes necessary. Mental health legislation through the Mental Health Act provides appropriately qualified individuals with the legal authority to treat people without consent for their own and the general public's protection (this is discussed at length in Chapter 7).

One aspect of the *National Service Framework* (Department of Health, 1999a) relates to the importance of collaborative working. Community Mental Health Teams (CMHTs) were commissioned in the 1980s. It is fair to say that mental illness places demands on services that cannot be met by one agency or discipline alone. *The Capable Practitioner* framework (Sainsbury Centre for Mental Health, 2001a) notes that the process of delivering mental health care requires working across a range of services in order to draw on the diversity of expertise and resources available. These include the legal system, social systems and political (policy) systems as well as the wider health and social services. Developing partnerships between health professionals, clients and carers is believed to be an important step forward in promoting effective working alliances in all the health services. Whilst many practitioners see the need for collaboration across services, it is not always easy. Despite numerous attempts at improving and coordinating services, through joint planning, restructuring, production of guidelines and refinement of procedures, there are countless examples of failure in collaboration, some of which attract media publicity. Hornby and Atkins (2000) argue that in addition to a structural approach to collaboration, a relational approach is also needed, one which is concerned with the human element of working together. One might argue that this is the bread and butter of a therapist's daily work, that is, the development of a collaborative alliance through a relational approach. But one could also question whether counselling and psychotherapy services are working in an integrative and seamless partnership with those that provide services to the mentally ill.

In the United Kingdom the government acknowledges in its 'Mental Health Policy Implementation Guide' (Department of Health, 2001) that few Primary Care Trusts provide the full range of mental health services. Typically, more specialised services are provided by Mental Health Trusts, and a variety of key services are provided by local councils as well as by the non-statutory sector and the charitable and voluntary sectors. With the number of different and differing agencies involved it is clear that the quality of collaboration between health and social care, statutory and non-statutory and voluntary services is of the utmost importance.

Currently a new integrated primary care liaison team is being piloted to replace the Community Mental Health Team. The aim is to provide services for patients with common mental health problems who require specialist interventions such as psychiatric or psychotherapeutic treatment. It is also the aim to provide support for those with more severe mental illnesses who cannot be supported in primary care alone. Whatever their title, it is envisaged that these new liaison teams, alongside primary care, will provide the key source of referrals to the newer teams.

It is recognised that in order for the new framework to operate effectively barriers between primary and secondary care and between health and social care should be tackled. To facilitate an effective partnership between health and social care, the Health Act of 1999 introduced powers enabling health authorities and local authorities to pool their budgets to commission and provide psychosocial interventions. This encouraged a multidisciplinary or interprofessional focus between for example, nurses, occupational therapists, general practitioners, social workers, health visitors, counsellors, psychologists and psychiatrists.

According to Mellor-Clarke (2000) there are now counsellors working in half of all general practices, and the government has set out clear guidelines on treatment choices including counselling and psychological therapies, although each local Primary Care Trust is developing its own protocol. It is perhaps part of the responsibility of counsellors working within or alongside the Health Service to familiarise themselves with these recommendations and the basic framework of change, in order that they too can contribute to an improved mental health service through increased collaboration.

Although it has been acknowledged in the *National Service Framework for Mental Health* that most mental health problems are managed in primary care and that one in four consultations with GPs are with people who have mental health problems, mental health receives only *41 of a possible 550* clinical points available to GPs in the new GMS contract (four per cent of the total). This seems inappropriately low. In addition to the low scoring and therefore low revenue, the majority of points that *are* available are awarded for performing annual checks. Three of the five mental health indicators are to do with patients on lithium therapy. Of the remaining two, one is a register of people with severe long-term mental illness and the other is a review, again of patients with severe long-term mental illness, linked to physical health, medication and secondary care. As with all quality frameworks this is linked to outcomes and, with mental health issues, measurable outcomes are hard to define. The exception to this is the quantitative recording of suicide statistics, the reduction of which has become the (inappropriate) focus of the *National Service Framework for Mental Health*. The huge amount of research conducted into areas such as psychological therapy since the mid-1960s has to a large extent failed to influence the design of either services or treatments (Parry, 1996). Such issues are addressed in depth in Chapters 6 and 7.

Labelling and stigma

In spite of the increased prevalence and incidence of mental health problems, mental illness is still surrounded by fear and misunderstanding and remains even now deeply taboo. Tudor (1996) notes that the history of mental illness is one of exclusion, separation, distinction and otherness. It is well known that the stigma and discrimination that is associated with mental health issues add to this experience of isolation, exclusion and distress (Mental Health Foundation, 2000). The Department of Health (2003) publication *Attitudes to Mental Illness* observed that attitudes towards people with mental health problems are often inconsistent and contradictory. Stereotyping, that is the belief that all people in a certain group conform to an unjustifiably fixed mental picture, is widespread and often leads to prejudice expressed through intolerance and ignorance. This is compounded by media stereotypes of individuals with mental illness, who are often portrayed as violent criminals.

Psychotherapists and counsellors do much to challenge the dominant discourses around psychiatric and mental illnesses. However, they can also, unintentionally, perpetuate the negative and uninformed views that lead to labelling, stigmatisation and subsequent isolation. This can simply be through lack of knowledge and understanding of the relationship of mental illness to their everyday clinical practice. The chapters that follow are therefore dedicated to providing a deeper appreciation of the wider influencing factors governing mental health, so that counsellors and other professionals who work in the psychological therapies can provide a more complete service to those experiencing mental distress.

CHAPTER 2

Understanding and assessing mental illness: The psychological aspects[1]

2.1 Psychiatrists and psychologists categorise mental illness. Are these categories helpful for counsellors?

Understanding and assessing mental health and illness are important aspects of the counsellor's everyday practice, and indeed can provide a framework for the client to make meaning of their experience. There has been a long held belief that clients' symptoms of mental distress can be categorised, although more recently this view has been contested. Psychiatrists and psychologists, in particular, have a tendency to diagnose mental illness according to the so-called 'medical model', which sees mental illness as a pathology, asserting that such a medical or scientific diagnosis is possible and that physical treatments can 'cure' the disease. Two examples of classification systems for mental illness according to this model are *The ICD-10 Classification of Mental and Behavioural Disorders* (World Health Organization, 1992) and *The Diagnostic and Statistical Manual of Mental Disorders (DSM-IV)*, published by the American Psychiatric Association (1994). The latter is the main diagnostic reference for mental health professionals in the United States of America and is a huge volume, designed, it seems, to satisfy the demands of the researcher and the lawyer, as much as the clinician. However, mental health and illness are complex and uniquely experienced phenomena and as such cannot easily be defined and categorised.

Counsellors themselves may well have different (and differing) views as to what constitutes mental illness. For example, mental illness may be seen as personal distress, the nature of which is individual. Such distress can be

---

[1] This chapter was written by Dawn Freshwater with contributions from Jeni Boyd.

examined in counselling and 'treatment' comes through increasing self-awareness and a willingness to challenge and change internal and external influences that contribute to the experience of distress. The counsellor or therapist does not view counselling as a 'cure', even though the client often arrives at the consulting room expecting one. This is sometimes called the 'psychotherapeutic model'. Some behaviourists view mental illness as forms of learnt behaviour conditioned by the individual's history, and 'treatment' is facilitated through behaviour modification. Other perspectives such as those taken from the 'sociological model' and the anti-psychiatry movement sees mental illness as part of the process of defining society (this is dealt with in more detail in Chapter 4). In whatever way mental illness is conceptualised, it is clear that counsellors need to be able to make an assessment of clients whose behaviour may appear bizarre, unpredictable and occasionally violent, in order to make decisions about the individual's suitability and receptivity to counselling as a process, and indeed their ability to maintain a therapeutic relationship.

Mental illness cannot always be clearly differentiated from what may be regarded as 'normal' behaviour. Distinguishing between bereavement and depression, or separating out an anxiety disorder from worry and work-induced stress is not straightforward. Whilst symptomatically the diseases may fall under the same diagnostic category, counselling would not only see these very differently but also find these labels unhelpful and possibly misleading. Some psychological theories rail against such categorisation and rigid diagnoses: Rogers, for example, thinks that 'psychological diagnosis as usually understood is unnecessary for psychotherapy, and may actually be a detriment to the therapeutic process' (1951, p. 220). He goes on to propose that the therapy itself is a form of diagnosis and that 'this diagnosis is a process which goes on in the experience of the client, rather than in the intellect of the clinician' (1951, p. 223).

For the client, the process of diagnosis or classification, using what are potentially concrete criteria (and subsequently stigmatising labels), may be seen as placing the locus of evaluation in the 'expert'. There is an inherent risk in this process of diagnosis and classification insofar as the client may expect the responsibility for understanding and 'curing' the problem to lie with the counsellor, rather than himself or herself. Other dangers include the potential for feelings of alienation and resistance, or of growing dependency on the counsellor in whom the client may invest the power to 'cure' their emotional distress. On the other hand, some clients may welcome a label as it gives a name, and therefore legitimacy, to their emotional distress. A diagnosis may provide a degree of relief for clients as it offers the possibility to talk about their distress and to share their experience with others, something they may not have felt able to do before. Counsellors may also derive a sense of security from a label, but only insofar as it appears to afford them a degree of control and authority over the client who carries it. Too often mental illness becomes something that belongs to others, rather than the counsellor (Freshwater, 2003). As Kendall notes:

> Our concept of ourselves as rational beings, guided by reason and intelligence, is crucial to our self confidence and self esteem; and encountering a fellow human being who has lost their reason and whose behaviour is no longer rational is profoundly disturbing, because it implies that the same might happen to us. (2001, p. 3)

One of the major disadvantages of diagnosis and categorisation is what I have referred to as labelling. Labelling can lead to stigma; and it is the stigma and the resulting feelings of guilt and shame, or the defensive denial that goes with it, that makes people with psychiatric symptoms reluctant to seek treatment, or even to accept that their symptoms exist and so might be a manifestation of mental disorder. Much has been written about labelling and stigma in psychiatry, particularly by the anti-psychiatrists (see for example Heller, Reynolds, Gomm, Muston & Pattison, 1996). Many clients report a huge resistance to the label of depression, for example, knowing that once the label has been pinned on them it will be harder to regain a sense of normality which will enable them to return to work. Difficulties obtaining employment that match their skills, securing a mortgage, emigrating or even obtaining holiday insurance can all be problematic once a firm diagnosis has been assigned. Overall there are still major issues regarding the acceptance of mental illness in society and one has to question whether the use of diagnostic categorisation helps or hinders efforts to 'normalise' experiences of mental distress that are common but often hidden (for further discussion of labelling, contrasted with the more positive concept of naming, see Jacobs, 1998, pp. 38–46).

The World Health Organization's (WHO) observation is a welcome one, that (in Europe at least) depressive illness ranks alongside ischaemic heart disease and cerebrovascular disease as one of the three leading contributors to the overall burden of disease (Murray & Lopez, 1997). It is important that mental illness is not perceived as the (stigmatised) behaviour of an apparent minority when in reality it is a common occurrence, and often merges seamlessly into what we regard as normality. Whilst this may not avoid the application of diagnostic categories, it becomes much harder to regard people with such labels as fundamentally different. Further, once recognised and accepted as a major health problem within the population, campaigns and policy initiatives begin to be taken seriously at all levels. For example, the profile of mental health has been raised by campaigns such as those of the Royal College of Psychiatrists, *Changing Minds* (1998) and 'Defeat Depression' (Paykel et al., 1997).

As we can see, defining mental illness is a complicated task and although the provision of a framework for thinking about mental illness and mental health may be useful to counsellors in general, it should be noted that definitions change over time and are influenced by society's views of what constitutes functional behaviour. At one end of a continuum is the ability to function in productive activities, to participate in meaningful relationships and to adapt and change in order to cope with any adversity. This is labelled mental *health*. Mental *illness* is characterised by impaired functioning due to alterations in thinking, mood or behaviour often associated with distress. Few people get through life without some impairment of functioning simply as a result of life circumstances; most find they can soon return to a level where they can work, have healthy relationships and perform daily tasks – a few, however, have more persistent difficulties and cannot return to their usual daily life without some form of treatment. Along this continuum there are various types and degrees of impairment with some disorders more severe than others. But even among individuals with the same diagnosis there is variation; the same classification of a mental illness may affect different people in different ways and even affect an individual differently at different times. It is these variations that counsellors are most often working with as opposed to the diagnostic label.

Nevertheless, it is true to say that most insurance companies and public insurance payers require a DSM-IV based diagnosis, which is aimed at, amongst other things, establishing consistency amongst practitioners before authorising types of treatment. The notion of classifications, such as those in the DSM-IV, are premised on objectivity and as such do not accommodate varying opinions or views. However, as Hauke points out, the objectivity of science is now questioned not because science is failing to meet its own standards but because 'a totally objective position is impossible to achieve. Any human examination of a phenomena [sic] must always involve human intervention into that phenomena [sic] which leaves it in a different state from before' (2000, p. 237).

Questions can be asked about the application of standardised treatments for standardised diagnoses, when in fact two unique individuals are creating a unique therapeutic alliance through the process of counselling. It is almost as if the application of criteria based diagnoses requires an objectivity that is incongruent with the subjective nature of counselling and therapeutic processes. In reality the application of any treatment is a subjective endeavour, as is the diagnosis of mental illness, albeit guided by 'evidence based' protocols.

Counselling not only takes into account this subjective involvement, it is predicated on it, acknowledging the inter-subjectivity that can be seen as contrasting sharply with the clinical classification that claims objectivity.

Truth and knowledge lead to the culture of the 'expert' who then becomes the legitimate authority. Western culture values the rationality of the medical profession, so the psychiatric profession, as a branch of medicine, is often seen as the profession that *knows* about diagnosis and about treatment. There is little room for alternatives, but knowledge is also linked to interest groups and much scientific 'knowledge', for example of depression, is driven as much by profit making by the research funders and the drug companies, as it is by a desire to understand. Drug manufacturers invest millions in research and development, not necessarily always out of philanthropy, but in pursuit of a marketable commodity that will boost profits (see also Chapter 4). Unfortunately, although there is a growing body of research that establishes the efficacy of counselling either alongside or as an alternative to medication, much of this is ignored or worse ridiculed because it does not fit the mechanistic and reductionist paradigm of medical science. Nevertheless, counsellors can take heart that in a recent Department of Health publication entitled *Organising and Delivering Psychological Therapies* (2004, p. 1) it is stated that 'psychological therapies are an essential part of health care. There is overwhelming evidence for their effectiveness in treating a wide variety of mental health problems and illnesses'.

For diagnostic guidelines to be of any use they also need to be practical and clear. According to the ICD-10, for example, common symptoms of depression include: reduced concentration and attention; reduced self-esteem and self-confidence; ideas of guilt and unworthiness (even in a mild type of episode); bleak and pessimistic views of the future; ideas or acts of self-harm or suicide; disturbed sleep and diminished appetite. How helpful is this labelling to counsellors when so many clients present with these symptoms? Many other factors need to be taken into consideration when diagnostic guidelines are being used, not least the context of the individual client.

It can also be argued that a medically based classification fails to differentiate between biological, emotional, psychological, sociological or environmental causes. Counsellors are more concerned with the aetiology of the problem as a way of understanding not only the causes but also teleologically where what treatment response can best be provided. Adhering to diagnostic categories may lead to the over-medicalisation of some everyday natural reactions to external circumstance that would in fact normally be considered 'coping mechanisms'.

In summary, counselling has tended to work from a 'growth' model rather than one of 'cure'. Criteria such as ego-strength, depth of damage, motivation and the patient's immediate environment (favourable or unfavourable) certainly have to be taken into account, alongside clients' experience of themselves. But counsellors and psychotherapists are more concerned with the *individual's* experience than with generalisations, and ask in what way such an experience, for example of anxiety or depression, interferes with life, relationships, productivity or happiness. As Carl Rogers observes 'The best vantage point for understanding behaviour is from the internal frame of reference of the individual himself' (1975, p. 258).

2.2   Some clients believe that their mental illness is hereditary. Is there any foundation for this belief?

There does appear to be a familial pattern to some forms of mental illness; for example, where there is a family history of schizophrenia and manic depression (also known as bipolar disorder) other family members may have a higher risk for developing a similar condition. However, the clearest finding from research is that there is no simple relationship between genes and mental disorders (NIMHE, 2005).

The Human Genome Project, begun in 1990, and originally planned for 15 years, accelerated its completion date to 2003. The result is a complete DNA sequence of every chromosome, revealing the position of every gene, enabling the identification of biologically significant changes in the genes that cause birth defects, cancer, cardiovascular conditions, diabetes, respiratory problems, muscular, skeletal and skin disorders and mental illness.

For some illnesses there are genetic tests to establish whether the relevant gene is present but this is not (as yet) the case for mental disorders. There are some frightening implications arising from this information; for example, if provided to insurance companies this may lead to discrimination in the cover provided, and in the hands of employers could affect a person's employment status. Labelling unfortunately leads to stigmatisation, prejudice and discrimination and may prevent some individuals from seeking help, thus strengthening the already deeply embedded narrative of diagnostic tools (see Question 2.1).

The evidence that heredity plays a role in the development of some forms of mental illness comes from comparing identical (monozygotic) twins who share 100 per cent of their genes and non-identical (dizygotic) twins who share only 50 per cent of their genes, like any biological siblings. If the rate of development is significantly higher among monozygotic twins then heredity is an important factor. However, some disorders have no genetic basis whilst others, for example Huntington's disease, have a clearly identifiable genetic factor. With regard to mental illness the idea of a single causative gene has been replaced by the concept of multiple genes, which, combined with non-genetic or environmental factors, lead to a predisposition to develop a disorder. This is called multifactoral inheritance, and schizophrenia and bipolar disorder are often cited as examples of this pattern.

A person may be able to determine if he or she is at particular risk by examining the family health history and discussing this with a medical practitioner. The consultation will probably focus on whether there is a known significant genetic contribution to the disorder, how closely related the person is to other affected family members and how many family members are affected. In the case of manic depression (bipolar disorder) there is a general population risk of 1–2 per cent of developing this disorder. In monozygotic twins, if one twin has bipolar disorder then the other twin also carries a 40–70 per cent risk factor. With non-identical twins the chance is 15–20 per cent, and with close relatives such as parents, children and siblings (first degree relatives) there is a 5–10 per cent chance of developing the disorder (NSW Genetics Education Program, 2003). While this is higher than for the general population these figures strongly suggest that heredity is not the *only* factor influencing the development of this form of mental illness; even if the gene (or genes) can be isolated and identified, this still only indicates a potential not a certain risk.

Many people are relieved to discover that there is a 'scientific' cause for their symptoms. However, as indicated in the answer to Question 2.1, the emphasis on establishing a scientific reason for a disorder can lead to the expectation of a scientific 'remedy', and further emphasis on pharmaceutical interventions. In addition to the biopsychological and sociopolitical problems around genetic research there are also a number of ethical, conceptual and philosophical concerns, particularly in relation to the notion of determinism and free will. It is interesting to note, for instance, that many individuals do not develop a disorder even when there is a statistically significant higher risk due to genetic inheritance.

Returning to the specific question asked by many clients, 'Is mental illness hereditary?' one might rightly associate the issue of heredity with legacy. Counsellors are not only concerned with biological or physical 'inheritance' but also with the socio-economic, philosophical, religious and emotional legacies provided by the individual's family, together with any psychological trauma (present or past), or environmental stress such as death, divorce, changing jobs or schools. Indeed, all the factors that form part of the complex pattern of the client's life may contribute to the risk of developing mental illness.

Different counselling approaches perhaps concentrate on exploring different areas of the client's life, but whatever theoretical background underpins a coun-sellor's practice, there is agreement generally that any idea arousing anxiety is always worth honouring with attention. What is important is the individual's perception of the situation, what the idea of mental illness means to them, their personal experience of mental illness within the family and their strengths (i.e. their resilience to the disorder) as well as the risks.

The philosophical issue of free will versus determinism may well be present in the more down to earth guise of responsibility. A diagnosis of illness being due to hereditary factors may disempower the client: it is genetic, therefore there is nothing they can do about it. Furthermore, the archetypal dyad of the invalid/healer is potentially polarised, with the result that the client looks externally to the medical expert, rather than working with the healer within. There is a danger too that this polarisation is mirrored and maintained by a split between those who believe in counselling and therapy, and those who believe that medication is the solution. Each instance should be decided on individually; there is undoubtedly a case for medication, for psychological therapies and for a combination of both (see Question 2.11).

In short, there is strong evidence for increased prevalence of diagnosis of some mental illness within families, but this does not 'prove' any heredity of mental illness. It is clear that the genetic predisposition to mental illness is an area that requires further systematic investigation before any firm conclusions can be made. Counsellors need to be aware of scientific developments as they emerge in order to establish a practice that is based on sound evidence and is well informed, but without losing sight of the fact that in most research findings what is put forward is only one part of the story.

2.3   A possible new client says at assessment that she is seeing a psychiatrist. What are the implications for me as her counsellor?

Many clients are referred to counsellors via a psychiatrist or as part of a wider treatment plan; conversely, counsellors may find themselves in the position of referring their clients to a psychiatrist. There are of course different responses to this question, depending on the setting within which the counsellor works. Whatever the setting, certain professional issues are inevitable, such as working collaboratively to facilitate the best treatment options for the individual client and concerns regarding confidentiality and clinical responsibility. It is not unusual for clients who are being managed in a community setting to have both a psychiatrist and a team of professionals supporting them in the primary care setting. For example, the community psychiatric nurse (CPN), general practitioner and practice counsellor often work together to enable an individual to remain in their own home. In these cases it is of the upmost importance that rigorous communication channels are maintained. This is not only a way of ensuring that the patient has the maximum support available, but is also a way of managing those professional concerns previously mentioned. Role clarification enables all parties, including the client, to ensure that boundaries and codes of practice are adhered too; regular case meetings should be held to avoid confusion. Role clarification and case conferences also assist in the identification of 'splitting' or 'manipulation' (a common feature of what is often labelled a personality disorder); or, more positively, the different aspects of the issue the client presents to different people, all of which can occur where more than one agency is involved, can be seen more as a whole. There are also advantages to working within a community mental health team or a psychiatric service, in that, when working with disturbed clients, the counsellor can draw on a great deal of support, and has more extensive knowledge of available services and how to access them.

For counsellors who are working in private practice, it is of course their own professional judgement and personal experience whether or not they work in conjunction with other outside agencies, such as psychiatric services. There are no hard and fast rules, and as such it basically comes down to personal preference and often to theoretical orientation. Of course, counsellors are encouraged to discuss all new clients with their supervisor before embarking on a therapeutic alliance, and where there is more than one treatment factor implied, it is all the more important to do so. Fundamentally, the implication for the counsellor here is the need for a clear and well thought out contract in order that the client can be contained in the most effective way that the system can provide.

Where a client is either making good progress or requiring additional treatment, it is important that feedback is provided for all practitioners involved in the case. It may occasionally be necessary for a client to temporarily suspend their work with the counsellor in order to concentrate on more pressing issues; and vice versa, a client may no longer require the help of a psychiatrist but wishes to continue to engage in counselling. Multidisciplinary working is sometimes viewed as a threat to the counselling frame; however, it carries with it the potential for more learning and is important for a holistic approach to client care. Chapter 6 examines the role of the multidisciplinary team and collaborative working in more depth.

2.4 If someone has a history of serious mental illness, are they likely to relapse when in counselling?

Counselling and psychotherapy can help individuals suffering from anxiety, panic, obsessional disorders, phobias, depression and other mental illnesses, where the person does not lose contact with reality and is able, with the support of a therapeutic relationship, to examine the possible origins of their problems. For some clients who have a history of severe mental illness counselling provides opportunities for readjustment and restoration. However, it may not be the best option for all clients and for some it may prove to be too difficult.

Counselling can uncover painful memories of events in the past that have not been resolved. Examples include bereavement, bullying and abuse (both as perpetrator and as victim) and other experiences that the client has not shared with others. Opening themselves up to the pain of talking about, or sometimes even re-living these experiences may generate different degrees of distress for the client. It is important, therefore, for clients to have the choice whether or not to work with those experiences, or whether to come back to them at a time when they feel more able to cope with the stress and anxiety they may produce. Although the counsellor may conclude that an event in the past may be contributing to a client's anxiety or depression in the present, it is the client's decision as to whether it is safe to examine this issue and whether he or she has the inner resources and support to deal with the strong emotions that may be generated. A client who has a history of mental illness should not automatically be precluded from counselling services, although it may be appropriate to provide additional support such as may be available from the community mental health service (see Question 2.3). Similarly, a client may wish to take leave from employment or seek support from someone close to them before embarking on such work. But it is not the client alone who makes the decision to work on painful issues. Counsellors also have to use their professional judgement collaboratively with the client to assist informed decisions about undertaking counselling in light of her or his previous history.

Whilst it is not necessarily the case that a client who has experienced a deep seated depression or a psychotic episode should be deemed unsuitable for counselling, it is important for the counsellor to be aware of other treatments that the client is undergoing, which may impact on their ability to make a therapeutic alliance. For example, if a client is currently taking anti-psychotic medication, it may still be possible to work with that person, although this has to be given serious consideration and should be discussed with the prescribing doctor, supervisor and other case workers involved. But it is important to be mindful of the consequences for the client if (as many clients do) they stop their medication at any point during the process (see Question 2.11). It is crucial to ensure that an explicit contract is developed when working with clients who have a history of mental illness, and that this contract is kept alive throughout the process.

As to the specific question of the likelihood of relapse, there is one particular disorder known as 'recurrent depression' that is prone to relapse, and which does not necessarily respond well to counselling. This disorder is characterised specifically by repeated episodes of depression, without any history of independent episodes of mood elevation, and by over-activity that fulfils the criteria of mania. (For more information see Mental Health Resources Centre www.nuts.cc/prob/depression.)

It is important to emphasise that when working with clients who have a history of mental illness a counsellor needs to be aware that relapse is a possibility. However, counsellors are always treading the line of uncertainty in knowing how a client might react to the therapeutic encounter. Whilst counselling may exacerbate an already existing problem, it has almost certainly not brought on the disorder. To a certain extent all counselling and psycho-therapy contains elements of relapse and regression. Horney writes of the ups and downs of therapy and how constructive periods are followed by what she calls repercussions or relapses, and suggests that these can be viewed as 'a definite move forward in a constructive direction' (1991, p. 359). For example, many people become more depressed in the initial phases of therapy, where their symptoms may be amplified. This is not always a bad thing; nevertheless a greater degree of containment may be required for both the client and the therapist.

2.5 Are there any contra-indications to counselling and psychotherapy where mental illness is concerned?

Individuals with a history of mild, moderate and severe mental illness can all benefit from counselling and psychotherapy. Therapy has a very valuable role to play in the treatment of both schizophrenia and manic depressive illness (see Question 2.4). Indeed more recently there have been many studies that indicate that short-term intervention therapies, specifically those based on a psychodynamic approach, can be successful in supporting clients who are diagnosed with their first episode of psychosis. Whilst individuals with a history of this type of disorder are usually treated in conjunction with anti-psychotic medication, counselling can help such clients overcome some of the consequences of the illness, whilst helping them to come to terms with those things that cannot be changed (SANE, 2003). Although many psychiatrists argue that medication is more effective than counselling for treating anxiety and depression, counselling remains the most frequently used form of treatment for these two common mental illnesses.

Counselling involves constant monitoring and evaluation; experience is underpinned by theory and intuition, and supported by training. Indeed, this reflection is part of a counsellor's everyday practice, leading to a continual assessment and evaluation of the therapeutic alliance, providing a vigilant attitude towards both the client and the counselling frame. This is part of counselling every client, not just those with 'mental illness', and it is not just at assessment that a counsellor is vigilant for emerging contra-indications.

In their practice counsellors are attuned on many levels to physical, emotional, conscious and unconscious signals manifest within the therapeutic field. When there is discord this can be registered consciously (and may or may not lead to an intervention at that point), or unconsciously, where a physical 'acting out' of this discord can be experienced in different parts of the body; or therapists may find themselves recognising that to take on a particular person does not feel right. Warning signals experienced in the counter-transference are hard to articulate and can be unsettling physically or emotionally: the therapist may feel a sense of threat with a client. These are not necessarily contra-indications to therapy, but they are signals to attend to. More explicit behaviours indicating a possible inability to create a therapeutic alliance include physical or verbal excitability, extreme agitation or withdrawal and inability to relate or engage in a relationship.

If a person is deluded, fantasising wildly or behaving in a way that is dangerous to self or others, if there are severe medical problems and no apparent resources to support the client, then the client may well be referred to secondary mental health services. This does not necessarily mean that counselling is inappropriate but that it needs to take place within a wider support network, and be conducted by an experienced counsellor (see Jacobs, 1999).

Physical appearance too can sometimes be an indicator. Does the client appear to be taking care of herself or himself? These signs are not always obvious and they do not always signify contra-indications. For example, sometimes people fear that they are 'going mad' when what they are experiencing is a flashback or abreaction, or when a particular emotion feels too strong to cope with, or when struggling to maintain a perspective on a life event.

It is the initial contact with a patient that often provides a good indicator of the client's ability to use the therapeutic alliance; thus skilful assessment is essential. However, even when counsellors feel well attuned and capable, they should also be constantly aware of their own limitations and their delusions of omnipotence. Where there is any doubt about the safety of the client or of the therapist supervision, alternative treatment should be sought.

2.6   How do I recognise that the client has an underlying mental illness that could be made worse by counselling or psychotherapy?

This question is closely linked to Questions 2.1 and 2.7 and relates back to the issues of categorising mental illness. As indicated in the answers to those questions, there are no straightforward signposts for detecting mental illness, just as there are no tried and tested markers by which the counsellor can measure the effectiveness of the counselling process. This is particularly the case in the early phases of the work where the client can often feel worse as they begin to articulate and express emotions that hitherto have been buried and denied. In addition, in the current climate, counsellors are taking on an increasingly diverse workload, meaning that the type and severity of pathologies encountered in the consulting room is much expanded. As Jacobs observes 'Counsellors are seeing clients, who some years ago would have been classified as beyond their skills and training. They have shown the capacity to work with such clients partly because there is no-one else available who can, and partly because the level of training in counselling, and their supervision, has greatly increased the wider application of counselling' (1999, p. 65).

A fundamental consideration when addressing the question of exacerbation of distress is to define the aim of the counselling in the first instance, that is to return to the contract and to what was originally negotiated. Egan (1990) suggests looking at the level of distress, and the uncontrollability and the frequency of symptoms as ways of judging the severity of the problem. These increases can be regarded as an indication that the problem is worsening. Being mindful of exacerbated symptomatology, however, needs to be balanced with simultaneous observation of the development of the alliance. The presence of 'primitive' defences such as splitting, idealisation or denigration may indicate an underlying mental illness, but these will not necessarily be made worse by counselling.

Although a client may not be 'made worse' by counselling, counselling may not be the most helpful strategy at this point in the client's life. For it to be helpful, clients need to be able to manage their own emotional responses and to work with the insights that can be generated through the therapeutic process. Substance abuse, chaotic lifestyles and severe physical illness amongst other things can interfere with the client's cognitive functioning and emotional processing, and may mitigate at that juncture against a therapeutic alliance between client and counsellor.

One barrier to recognising that counselling may not be the most appropriate strategy for the client is the counsellor's own need to be helpful. Wanting to 'rescue' the client may become a more powerful driver for the counsellor than listening to the cues provided in the therapeutic relationship.

2.7 Are there any existing frameworks for assessing a client's mental health?

Assessing a client's mental health is part of a counsellor's scheme of practice, to ensure, amongst other things, that the most appropriate client care can be offered. However, models and structures of assessment may not always be explicit. Initial assessment of the client's suitability for counselling is carried out for a number of reasons; nevertheless it might be worthwhile reflecting on both why clients need to be assessed and what is being assessed. Further, it is important to reflect on the structure and type of assessment used. The reason for such questions is that assessment can be driven, particularly within organisations, by a number of internal and external socio-economic and political agendas. For example within the NHS, which is constantly struggling to balance cost effectiveness with high-quality appropriate care, assessment is often linked to determining the shortest time necessary to effect treatment and restore functionality.

Assessment is of course ongoing and continuous in counselling, where working with clients means counsellors assessing and evaluating themselves and their responses, together with their client's ability and willingness to work with particular interventions. One of the most important components is self-assessment. How competent and confident does the counsellor feel in dealing with the client and their presenting problems? Can he or she support the client through a sustained period of deconstruction?

Assessment is also a two-way process: clients will be assessing the counsellor during the initial meeting, perhaps directly by asking questions about confidentiality, how therapy works, length of time and many other factors, and certainly intuitively, judging trustworthiness, integrity, expertise and whether they feel comfortable enough to talk openly. Assessment is also about building the early stages of the therapeutic alliance. Clients may well come with certain expectations, for example, of a quick fix, or fears such as that they will be labelled 'mad', or even that seeing a counsellor is 'mad', all of which are relevant to explore in the early phases of the work.

Many counsellors seem to have their own models of assessment, some of which are rather individualistic, but there are some common threads. Fundamental and routine questions often asked during informal or formal assessment include the presenting problem and how it is experienced, the frequency of the problem, and recent factors precipitating referral, whether there are underlying or associated problems, whether other help has been sought currently or in the past and if the client is taking medication. All of this is of course linked to observations from non-verbal communication such as appearance and manner of presenting, facial expression, posture, pitch and tone of voice and so on. A psychosocial history often emerges as life events and social and economic circumstances are explored, including adverse life situations such as abuse, violence, accident or illness. Some counsellors and therapists prefer to take such a history rather than waiting for it to emerge. Most commonly, therapists combine waiting for the client to describe their history, while asking judicious questions at certain points, in order to clarify or open up the picture. Assessment also identifies those not suitable for counselling and psychotherapy. But since this requires that the counsellor makes a judgement of the client's mental health, assessment tools might assist in this process, even if they are only one part of the picture.

Most counsellors are not trained 'experts' in the field of mental health but are trained to work with people who are experiencing the type of difficulties and problems in their lives that are interfering with their day-to-day functioning, ranging from depression and anxiety, stress at work, grief over the death of a loved one or relationship difficulties to a more general lack of purpose in life. Clients may also be referred for counselling, particularly within primary care, as non-urgent cases who might like to see (or would more appropriately be treated by) a psychiatrist but are unlikely to get an appointment for some months. To this end, counsellors should also view the assessment process as a time during which referral to other external agencies can be determined (see Chapter 6).

In addition to the diagnostic tools mentioned in 2.1, there are many existing frameworks that purport to measure and assess mental health: see, for example *Finding depression in primary care* (http://www.jr2.ox.ac.uk/bandolier/ band99/b99-6.html), which provides a clear account of the latest diagnostic criteria for depression and up-to-date information on the performance of various simple screening and diagnostic systems for primary care. Common instruments of assessment can be located in a number of places (Williams, Noel, Cordes, Ramirez & Pignone 2002). Screening questionnaires can be useful as a tool to assist diagnosis, to monitor clinical progress or to differentiate between somatic and psychological pain. Current screening questionnaires include the General Health Questionnaire, the Hospital and Anxiety Depression Scale, the Geriatric Depression Scale, the Edinburgh Postnatal Depression Scale and the Beck Depression Inventory. However, different schools of psychological thought usually advocate their own assessment instruments, including psychometric tests and various anxiety and depression scales. Whilst there is no shortage of assessment tools, the reliability and validity of these tools has not necessarily been ascertained, making it difficult to know exactly what is being measured.

Burton (1998) emphasises the differences between therapy models and professional disciplines in terms of assessment, arguing that some models may pay more attention to the sequence of feelings, some to the words or metaphors used, some to the physical experience of the symptomology and some to the actual relationship that is developing. She goes on to say that 'psychodynamic and humanistic models of psychotherapy are closer in emphasis to one another than either of them is to CBT'. In relation to assessment, however, she writes, 'the major difference from our standpoint occurs in the matter of assessment: person-centered therapists often do not make a detailed initial assessment, whereas assessment is an essential part not only of the psychodynamic formulation but also of the cognitive–behavioural working hypothesis and the sequential diagrammatic reformulation of cognitive–analytic therapy' (Burton 1998, p. 83). She suggests that a detailed assessment of a client's mental state in primary care can help to avoid inappropriate brief treatment, which may lead to no improvement or worse to relapse; to avoid repeated referrals to and subsequent rejections from the varying secondary services; and to avoid missing long undiag-nosed severe mental illness. She also declares that sometimes the initial interviews for assessment require 3–6 hours on as many days. Although she says they can occasionally be completed in an hour, one wonders just how realistic this is, given the current climate of increased throughput and waiting list initiatives.

A recent study of three brief, self-rating instruments of assessment was carried out to compare the different methods of identifying depression in primary care. One of the existing frameworks surveyed was disorder-specific [the depression module of the Brief Patient Health Questionnaire (B-PHQ, nine items)]; one was broad based [the General Health Questionnaire (GHQ-12, 12 items)]; and one was less restricted to both issues (WHO-5 Well-being Index WHO-5, five items) (see also Henkel et al., 2003). The findings of the study suggest that the use of WHO-5 could improve the family doctor's ability to detect depression. The findings also support the World Health Organization's recommendation that every patient in primary care should participate in a screening process, with the completion of WHO-5 as a standard first step, a questionnaire that can be completed in the waiting room. There are also many commonly used assessment scales, and several screening instruments for depression. Such forms appear quite regularly in population health surveys, see, for example, the Carroll Rating Scale for Depression (Carroll, Feinberg, Smouse, Rawson & Greden, 1981); a self-administered version of the Hamilton Rating Scale for Depression (Hamilton, 1967); the General Health Questionnaire (Goldberg, 1972, 1978), which despite its title is a measure of psychiatric symptoms, predominantly depression; the Beck Depression Inventory (Beck, Ward, Mendelson, Mock & Erbaugh, 1961); and the Zung Self-Rating Depression Scale (Zung, 1965).

Although some counsellors may feel that formal assessment procedures go counter to the ethos of a non-directive therapeutic relationship, perhaps (especially with time-limited counselling) they need some way of formalising and checking their intuitive assessment. With a waiting list and scarce resources some form of assessment is necessary, particularly as an attempt needs to be made to free counselling from the role of being regarded as only a stopgap. Generally assessment can be made along two axes. On one axis there is the concept of distress, which can be ranked on a simple continuum from normal through neurotic to borderline and psychotic. But one of the difficulties counsellors face is that clients may present, or be referred, in the prodomal phase of a psychosis, exhibiting signs of anxiety, irritability or depression, having difficulty concentrating or remembering, being pre-occupied with ideas, or having a loss of energy and lack of sleep resulting in social withdrawal and difficulty functioning. All of these can be present without necessarily being an indication of incipient psychosis. Assessment of these behaviours is dependent on the counsellor's tacit knowledge, as well as on both their theoretical knowledge and the expertise of the supervisor and/or other team members.

The second axis represents the ability to relate to the counsellor, having some degree of psychological understanding and insight into problems, together with a positive view of the possibility of improvement. People who cannot relate, or who see all problems as the fault of others, who have been 'told to come' by their GP or their partner, who stigmatise mental health issues, or who have poor motivation through cultural expectation or social circumstance may be less suitable for counselling. In reality the 'cut' has to be made in the public sector or through other voluntary organisations; but in private practice the decision may not be so easy, particularly as the counsellor's livelihood may depend on it.

Another important aspect of any assessment, whether formal or informal, is risk assessment. Opportunity needs to be created for some gentle discussions around suicidal feelings, self-neglect, self-harm, aggression towards others and other third party risks. Currently there is no legal requirement in this country to enforce treatment or prevent suicide but with the *National Service Framework for Mental Health* (Department of Health, 1999a) outlining plans for reducing the suicide rate, a protocol for assessing suicide risk may well be required by a managed service. A 'risk clause' should be included in the client contract, although it has been argued that even 100 per cent improvement in risk assessment would identify only 30 per cent of suicides, and there would still be the problem of finding effective resources.

Counsellors working in primary care, for Employment Assistant Programmes or for other organisations may find a standard assessment procedure already in place. The Beck Depression Inventory and GHQ-12 are two of the most popular measures, although the evidence to support them is limited. The current emphasis on outcome measures of efficacy as a way of justifying funding means that pre- and post-treatment assessment and evaluation forms are becoming more widespread. One example is CORE, an abbreviation for Clinical Outcomes for Routine Evaluation (www.coreims.co.uk), which is the first standardised public-domain approach to audit, evaluation and outcome measurement for UK psychological therapy and counselling services. It concerns itself with four key areas: subjective well-being (current level of distress and self-esteem), problems or symptoms, life or social functioning and risk to self or others.

Co-ordinated by the Psychological Therapies Research Centre at the University of Leeds, CORE was developed between 1995 and 1998 by a multidisciplinary team of researchers and practitioners, who represented the major psychological therapy professions. Nevertheless, difficulties can arise when assessment gets confused with evaluation tools and outcome measures. CORE itself is both an initial screening tool and an outcome measure, but is often used only for its evaluative component.

In summary, currently assessment is carried out in a rather ad hoc way in the NHS, in managed services and in primary care, with referral criteria not being consistent within practices, let alone between them.

2.8 What is the difference between endogenous depression and reactive depression? Does it make a difference as to whether counselling is effective?

The question of whether depression has biological roots or is a reaction to life events is one that has been debated for decades. Recent research suggests that the majority of depressive disorders result from a failure to meet goals derived from evolutionary based needs. However, as Brown (1996, p. 37) points out, 'gaps between goals and their fulfilment must generally have particular qualities for clinical depression to emerge'. Further studies consistently fail to demonstrate any significant difference in endogenous and non-endogenous conditions. Thus, the traditionally polarised viewpoint of depression as either endogenous or reactive is being challenged, as a more balanced understanding of the interrelationship of life events, genetic factors and psychosocial influences emerges. Whilst there is little doubt about the existence of an endogenous depression, life events play a significant role in all types of depression. Several studies link major life losses with the experience of depression, with estimations that as many as 75 per cent of severe events leading to depression involve a loss (Finlay-Jones, 1989). Indeed as Chesler (1996, p. 51) observes: 'depression is a response to loss either of ambivalently loved other, the ideal self, or of meaning'.

An endogenous depression is viewed predominantly as biologically caused, arguably due to either genetic causes (see Question 2.2) or a malfunction in the brain chemistry. However, all depression involves some changes in brain chemistry, even when the cause is clearly a psychological trauma. Chemical changes occur in certain pathways of the brain and may be different in various forms of depression. Whether these changes are the cause of the depression, rather than one of its consequences is heavily contested. Franklin (2003) argues that sometimes endogenous depression is used as a label to describe people who do not respond well to treatment, and at other times is a rationale to prescribe medication, without offering any psychological treatment.

Reactive depression is defined as depression that occurs in response to some specific and identifiable psychosocial stressor. Symptoms of a reactive depression are similar to other depressive disorders, and because of the relationship between the symptoms and a specific stressor there may be more emphasis on a problem-solving approach, which might involve making concrete changes in lifestyle or working patterns and may require specific actions and decision making. Once the type of depression has been identified, specific treatment options may be prescribed.

For counsellors one of the fundamental questions is whether the distinction between endogenous and reactive depression influences the decision about the appropriateness of counselling as an intervention. Talking treatments are in fact appropriate for all types of depression, providing the client is able to use the relationship and engage in the counselling process. There is some evidence to suggest that the most promising treatments currently available are cognitive–behavioural therapy, interpersonal therapy and problem-solving therapy (Depression Alliance 2003). Armstrong (1997) points out that targeted counselling is most useful for helping people with depression. If it is seen as endogenous then there may be less hope that clients may feel disempowered as a result of the label (see Question 2.1) and be less willing to work with a therapist, since the locus of control is experienced as beyond their own influence.

Perhaps the most relevant area to explore with a prospective client is their own perception of their depression: if it can be ascribed to a concrete event or events then there may be a more positive expectation of ultimate successful resolution through counselling.

2.9   Should I work with someone who has severe depression?

Severe depression is usually associated with chronicity, both in relation to the length of time that the client has lived with the illness and previous attempts at effecting treatment. As with all clients, those referred with depressive disorders need to be given a full and detailed assessment of their ability and willingness to work with the therapeutic alliance.

Specific questions that might reflect or determine whether or not to work with an individual include:

- Is the client sufficiently motivated?
- Is the client responsive and able at least to begin to articulate how they are feeling?
- Do therapist and the client have realistic expectations with regard to the effect of counselling on the depression?
- Does the client believe that counselling can make a difference?
- Does the client have a supportive social and/or family network?
- Is the client taking prescribed medication and what effect will this have on their cognitive functioning?
- What is the client's relationship to their depressive illness?
- What is the family history in relation to mental illness?

Short-term counselling *can* be useful in helping to overcome the debilitating symptoms of severe depression and help the individual get back to a functioning life. It cannot, however, address the underlying problems and in many cases what is not dealt with will return in the future with increased severity. It may not be helpful or indeed possible for clients who are profoundly depressed to work with painful past experiences. In such cases it may be more helpful to work on strategies to help individuals to regain a sense of their own agency, whilst acknowledging that dealing with deep-seated issues at a later date may be important in order to help them cope with recurring low mood, high levels of anxiety or stressful situations in the future.

2.10   Is it true that psychotherapy doesn't work with psychotic clients?

Schizophrenia is the commonest form of psychosis, with symptoms including thought disorders, hallucinations and delusions. The other main psychotic illness is bipolar affective disorder (often referred to as manic depression), in which the main features are extreme changes of mood. The causes of psychotic illnesses are not well understood, although there are usually abnormalities in the chemistry of the brain (see Question 2.8) that are thought to cause changes in thoughts, feelings and behaviours (Royal College of Psychiatrists, 2002).

For some people a psychotic episode may be an acute, one-off event triggered by a physical illness (psychosis is common in clients following a period in intensive care units) or a stressful event. For others psychotic symptoms appear to have been with them for most if not all of their lives, necessitating in-patient care. The question of whether counselling and psychotherapy is effective with this client group does not have a straightforward answer and is related to the underlying cause of the psychosis. The counsellor, and other involved and interested agencies, need to work closely with the client on the goals of the therapy, should it be appropriate. When working with clients who have experienced psychosis over a period of time, treatment can really only aim to reduce the symptoms of the illness, hopefully preventing them from recurring, and helping to restore a normal life. Medication plays an important role in the management of psychosis and usually needs to be taken for some time. However, other forms of treatment are also important. Through counselling such clients can at least experience being heard, respected and listened to with care and consideration.

Theorists approach the suitability of therapy with psychotic clients from a variety of viewpoints. Carl Jung, for example, preceded the well-known work of RD Laing in his interest in patients with dementia praecox, now commonly referred to as schizophrenia. Jung always placed an emphasis on what was experienced by each individual, paying particular attention to the content of dreams, hallucinations or seemingly random speech. He established that these were significant psychic products, not ramblings of the insane, and that contained within these were symbols of the distress. By taking these utterances seriously he looked further at the psychology of the illness and this brought some relief to his patients at the Burgholzli Clinic, although he did not aim to 'cure'. As Samuels, Shorter & Plaut note, Jung viewed schizophrenia 'as a psychosomatic disorder where changes in body chemistry and in personality were somehow connected or linked. At the time of his student days Jung's superior Bleuler thought that a toxin produced by the body led to psychological disturbance. Jung's crucial contribution was to estimate the importance of Psyche sufficiently to reverse the elements: psychological activity may lead to somatic changes' (1987, p. 133). This was revolutionary thinking at the time.

2.11 How effective are psychological therapies with clients who are on medication for mental illness?

In reality counsellors and therapists today work with many people who are taking (or have recently taken) prescribed medication for what may be classified as 'mental illness'. Medication, as already indicated, is a convenient (and often effective) treatment to administer; it may enable the client to engage in the therapeutic alliance in a way that would not otherwise be possible. As such it is important to understand how medication may affect the client and subsequently the counselling process. Some counsellors believe that the underlying assumption in counselling (that clients have their own internal resources to find solutions to their problems) is contrary to the idea of taking medication. Others perhaps see prescribed drugs as necessary exterior scaffolding whilst inner strength is restored. Such responses are likely, at least in part, to depend on the theoretical orientation of the counsellor. Those with a cognitive or behavioural approach may be less concerned if medication is blocking off feelings than those whose approach particularly emphasises the expression of emotions and feelings, where medication designed to suppress worry and anxiety may limit the client's ability for such expression.

Even this may be too simplistic, because each individual reacts differently to the medication and will have specific concerns about the drugs prescribed. A well-informed counsellor can help a client explore many of the issues and concerns around medication and in doing so contribute to the building of a trusting therapeutic relationship. This may be necessary before work with other underlying problems can begin, but counselling should be led by the client's needs rather than the counsellor's expectations. However, a judgement has to be made as to the client's ability to decide whether or not to engage in counselling, and the ability to reflect in a useful way on that process, and whether that is impaired by taking medication. If thinking and feeling are very disrupted then counselling may have to wait.

Of course, clients may be on medication for many reasons other than just mental illness: clients who have acute or chronic physical illnesses, or are having treatment for terminal illness, will invariably be receiving pharmaceutical intervention. These are just as likely to influence the individual's ability to utilise the therapeutic alliance as is an antidepressant or antipsychotic drug.

Medications that are likely to be prescribed for mental illness include antidepressants, antipsychotics, anxiolytics and hypnotics. Betablockers are also sometimes prescribed for severe anxiety; they act by blocking the noradrenaline released as the result of anxiety and by blocking beta-receptors located in the heart muscle, airways and blood vessels.

Hypnotics and anxiolytics are prescribed to improve sleep, but people who are not mentally ill also have periods of time when they do not sleep well. Counselling can help here by discussing the individual's sleep expectations: older people need less sleep and sometimes other causes are underestimated. Alternative relaxation and sleep techniques can be explored and support can be offered through the difficulties. Hammersley and Beeley (1992), in their paper 'The effect of medication on counselling', suggest that long-term use of these drugs can lead to difficulty in thinking constructively, together with feelings of dependence on the prescribed drug. In addition, hypnotic induced sleep tends to consist of less REM sleep, and when the drugs are withdrawn there may be an excess of dreams and nightmares, which can be very disturbing. As with most things if this is understood and talked about it can be tolerated and worked through.

Currently hypnotics are often prescribed to help cope with bereavement, as the sedative properties help the management of acute stress, panic, grief or anxiety. Many counsellors see bereavement as a normal grief reaction that although long and painful should not be pathologised. Some individuals have dysfunctional reactions to grief and may need medication, but the tendency seems to be routine prescription rather than encouragement to allow expression of the thoughts and feelings, with support from counsellors during this time.

Antipsychotics (sometimes referred to as neuroleptics) have been found to be effective in treating the most disturbing forms of psychotic illness such as schizophrenia and manic depression. The effectiveness of the antipsychotics has been proved by extensive research but like all medications they have their limitations and side effects. As with hypnotics, they are not a cure, merely a way of treating some of the symptoms. However this is important because it may make the difference between leading a near normal life and being institutionalised. Side effects are not easy to predict since they depend not only on the particular antipsychotic and the dose prescribed, as well as on the person's susceptibility, which may vary greatly. This makes it very difficult for counsellors and therapists who work with clients taking this type of medication, since it is hard to discern the symptoms of the illness from the side effects of the medication.

According to MIND the prescribing of antidepressants more than doubled during the 1990s: 'In 1991, nine million prescriptions for anti-depressants were written in England. By 2000, the number had reached 22 million' (Health Which, 2002). Perhaps this is not surprising given that depression is the most common form of 'mental illness'. Taken regularly, it is thought that antidepressants contribute to the recovery of 70 per cent of patients, preventing recurring episodes of depression in those with severe pathology (Depression Alliance, 2003). There are three main classes of antidepressant drugs:

1. Monoamine oxidase inhibitors (MAOIs): these are not often used currently because of their reaction with certain food types, known as the 'cheese effect'.
2. Tricyclics: the original modern antidepressant, used frequently, but causing troublesome side effects and dangerous if taken in an overdose.
3. Selective serotonin re-uptake inhibitors (SSRIs): a relatively recent addition to the group of medications used as antidepressants and showing many advantages over the earlier tricyclics, particularly with regard to side effects.

It is worth mentioning that St John's Wort (hypericum), a herbal remedy which has been known for thousands of years, has recently been produced in tablet form, and extensively marketed as a treatment for depression. Many people are under the impression that herbal remedies are 'natural', and this means that they are completely safe and free of side effects. Clients may not realise that hypericum interacts with a number of conventional drugs such as warfarin or the birth control pill, and may not tell their doctor that they are taking this product. Here a counsellor could be an important source of information. Significantly, it should not be taken at the same time as SSRIs or MAOIs; in fact it has been made a prescription-only drug in the Irish Republic because of anxieties about its possible similarity to MAOI antidepressants.

It is also important that counsellors are aware that tricyclic antidepressants are extremely toxic. If working with clients who are expressing suicidal thoughts and where their doctor has prescribed a tricyclic antidepressant to alleviate symptoms, they have to hand a ready means of suicide. The risk of suicide often accompanies depression (Davies, Naik & Lee, 2001); and as Healy (1993, p. 84) explains: 'It has been widely noted that one of the times people are most likely to kill themselves has been around 10–14 days after starting anti-depressant treatment'. He cites various possible reasons as to why this should be the case, such as an increase in drive and energy before retardation of suicidal thoughts, dissociative reactions that lead to feelings of hopelessness and of being 'incurable', impaired sexual functioning and fear of permanent damage.

There is also evidence that some of the most popular antidepressants interfere with sexual functioning. This may be one area of concern that is brought to the counsellor's attention. In men, antidepressants may cause difficulties in sustaining an erection or in ejaculating. However, there are no accurate figures available to estimate the extent of the problem, which is complicated by the fact that a reduction in libido is a symptom of depression itself. The effect of medication on the sexual functioning of women is also less clear, as most of the studies carried out are gender biased, but frequency and intensity of menstruation may be disturbed, there may be breast tenderness, orgasmic difficulties and increased or decreased libido.

Although purists may say that counsellors should not give advice, therapists are concerned with the whole person, and if a client has concerns about dosage, side effects or withdrawal from medication it can be helpful to discuss this with a counsellor before consulting their doctor. Counsellors can give information, ask clarifying questions and give some indication of what to expect (whilst still recognising individual differences), all with the aim of empowering the client. In addition to noting the type of medication prescribed, a vigilant and observant counsellor will note how important the drugs are to the client. Do they, for example, think that the restoration of their self-confidence is due, in some way, to the medication? Thinking this way could lead to the belief that they need to continue taking the tablets to remain stable and so is likely to undermine the client's confidence in their own resources.

Many people express a desire to end medication, or are concerned about ending it, and it should be emphasised to the client that the counsellor is not medically qualified and that such concerns should also be discussed with the prescribing doctor. It also needs to be noted that many people do not take the pills prescribed for them, either because their illness appears to be cured, or because they do not like the side effects produced by the drug. The greater the side effects experienced the more difficult their compliance. People who are severely depressed can often see no point in being helped, and anxious patients may be so overcome by worry that they forget the medicine altogether. Counsellors have to remember that although a medication has been prescribed, it is not necessarily taken. Sometimes clients say that they have stopped (or never taken) the tablets, without consulting their GP, and so some knowledge of the effects of stopping drugs may be useful. This came to the fore with the much publicised doubts about Seroxat, where the coroner expressed concern that it was 'a dangerous drug that should be withdrawn until at least detailed national studies are undertaken' (*Daily Mail*, 14 March 2003). This led to patients questioning their GPs and therapists about the safety of antidepressants and medication in general.

In summary, many clients present for counselling whilst taking prescribed medication, which leads to complex interactions between mind and body, with the hormonal systems, the nervous system and the many neurotransmitter chemicals being affected by the antidepressants. The difficulty with any medication prescribed for mental illness is that, although symptoms may be alleviated, it generally does nothing about the underlying cause of distress. There are also many socio-economic factors to be taken into consideration, for example unemployed people are twice as likely to suffer from depression as people in work; children in the poorest households are three times more likely to have mental health problems than children in the best off households; and suicide is three times higher in young Asian women (Hudson-Allez, 2003) (see also Chapter 4). Medication cannot change these social dynamics, but, along with counselling, it may provide the individual with an opportunity to find ways of leading a more satisfying and fulfilling life. Medication alone does not solve problems; drugs cannot give insight into relationships, improve communication or teach coping strategies. But medication may allow the individual to cope sufficiently with day-to-day life so that counselling can play an increasing role in the development of their mental health.

CHAPTER 3

Psyche and soma: The relationship between mental health and physical symptoms[1]

3.1 What is the relationship between physical illness and mental illness?

The interrelationship of mental illness and physical health is a complex and multifaceted one. Many people at some point in their lives have a serious illness. Both the illness and the treatment for it can affect the way we think and feel. The sudden onset of an illness or a physical injury may be experienced as an overwhelming disruption of the way individuals usually relate to their own body and to their world. The effect of chronic illness is equally profound. Loss of control over bodily functions is experienced as particularly distressing and shameful, like the involuntary opening of bowels or bladder, the inability to walk or to do small things for ourselves such as washing or feeding ourselves. Mental and physical illnesses are frequently found together in the same individual (Meltzer, Gill, Petticrew & Hinds, 1995) and as such counsellors and therapists are more likely than not to be faced with individuals who are experiencing both physical and psychological distress. In the guide to managing mental illness for general practitioners published by the Sainsbury Centre for Mental Health (2001b), it is argued that the percentage of people with mental illness and physical co-morbidity is high (many individuals with mental illness have poor diets, are heavy smokers and do not take exercise). Importantly, information on the frequency with which health status information is recorded in patients' records suggest that it is much lower than for other groups of patients, making it difficult to assess the degree to which patients with mental illness experience concurrent physical ill health. Some specific data is available regarding people diagnosed with

---

[1] This chapter was written by Dawn Freshwater with contributions from Jeni Boyd.

schizophrenia and bipolar disorder: they are known to suffer from an increased risk of cardiovascular disease, respiratory disease, diabetes and drug related movement disorders (Harris & Barraclough, 1998).

Despite the fact that the mind and body have traditionally been separated in Western thought, it has long been known that the psychological and emotional states of human beings influence their physical health, and conversely that the physical state of a person affects the mind. Scientists have spent many years attempting to unravel and make sense of the relationships between the mind (psyche) and body (soma), understanding that disease rarely has one single cause. In the postmodern era the 'medical model' and its approach to sickness and recovery have been seriously questioned. Further, Descartes's description of the person, composed of a separate 'mind' and 'body', has been challenged, resulting in an increasing acceptance of the holistic model. To a certain degree these changes were pre-empted by the work of Winnicott, which acknowledged that psyche and soma are not separable entities but inseparable aspects of a singular psychical organism, thus paving the way for some new possibilities in psychotherapeutic intervention.

There has not always been agreement regarding the extent to which the mind and body are interrelated and even today we are faced with conflicting messages, both within health care and society in general. On the one hand there is almost uncritical acceptance of alternative and complementary therapies by those who firmly believe that the mind is both the source and the remedy for the majority of physical diseases. Consequently, there has been an exponential growth of alternative therapies since the mid-1980s, all of which tend to emphasise the unity of mind and body. Other, more sceptical onlookers, either dismiss the connections between psyche and soma, or simply ignore them altogether. As Martin (1997, p. 9) comments: 'Psychosomatic phenomena carry with them a whiff of self-indulgent fantasy, along with the implication that they lack both substance and scientific respectability'. The dominance of the medical model and its disease oriented approach to managing health and illness has meant that the patient's emotions and mental state have increasingly come to be seen as irrelevant. And of course it is, apparently, easier to seek and find physical causes for illness such as cholesterol levels, bacteria, viruses and so on. Whilst all of these may be important contributory factors to the client's current condition, they do not tell the whole story. Additionally the stigma of mental illness means it is still easier to talk about physical illness, particularly in certain age groups (see Question 2.1).

As mentioned in Question 2.7, psychotherapists seek to understand the outward physical, verbal and behavioural signs of an individual's felt 'dis-ease' in order to care. Physicians, in the main, seek to interpret bodily symptoms as signs of some organic disease in order to 'cure'. Freshwater (1998) argues that psychological suffering often manifests itself in the form of physical symptoms, which could signal the psyche's unconscious way of drawing attention to the inner tension or conflict that would otherwise be ignored at a psychological and emotional level. This is based on the belief that all disease has an inherent meaning. The term pathology, for example, when traced back to its Greek origins, translates into suffering (*pathos*) and meaning (*logos*). It is worth noting that the term *katharsis* can also be traced back to ancient times, where it was used to refer to the purging and purification of the person's soul. Freud, of course, was an early exponent of psychosomatic medicine, linking physical symptoms to unconscious emotional conflicts. Jung (1968) also envisaged the body as inextricably linked with the mind, extending this idea to include the collective unconscious. He writes of the body as being an expression of the 'physical materiality of the psyche', viewing psychosomatic symptoms as potentially creative with a teleological value. Samuels et al. (1986) suggest that many aspects of the 'shadow' are concentrated in the body and an acceptance of the body is absolutely necessary for psychological development.

Carla van der Moolen (2002, p. 451) also considers the interaction between the psychological and somatic processes, stating: 'One of the basic principles of client-centred psychotherapy is that people can overcome process stagnation and can get in touch with their inner experience by concentrating on the felt sense. The felt sense is not a mental but a physical experience. Only the body is fully aware of how problems feel and what their essence is'. Existentialist Eugene Gendlin (1990) argues for the unfolding wisdom of the body, sensing that meaning can be directly felt in an embodied way.

Viktor Frankl, a clinician as well as a philosopher, saw the human being as an entity consisting of: body (soma), mind (psyche) and spirit (noetic core). He suggested that we can experience sickness in the body and the mind, but the human spirit, our noetic core, remains healthy, although access to that healthy core can be blocked. He suggests that we should look to the healthy spiritual core of man for sources of healing, instead of analysing and pathologising (Frankl, 1984) (see Chapter 5).

Often clients seem to make clear that there is something deeply troubling them through their body but they do not understand this at a psychological level and so focus on the physical complaints. This may be met with frustrating encounters with the medical profession whose tests and procedures can 'find nothing of note'. As a last resort they may be referred to the counsellor, suspicious and resentful or fearful that they are 'mad'.

As such the disciplines of counselling and psychotherapy have grown up with a theory, even if somewhat misleading, of the body–mind connection. Hauke quotes a footnote that first appeared in the 1927 English translation of *The Ego and the Id*: 'The ego is first and foremost a bodily ego' (2000, p. 181). That is to say that the ego is ultimately derived from bodily sensations and may be regarded as a mental projection of the surface of the body. In our

Western culture it is apparent how the body takes over the expression of the ego: witness the overemphasis on body image, cosmetic surgery, body piercing and tattoos, eating disorders and indeed self-harm.

Culture is certainly an influential factor when considering the link between physical and psychological disease. Shorter (1994) believes that some people are born with a biological predisposition to respond to stress, for example through physical symptoms that have no apparent physical cause, suggesting that the particular symptoms that a person manifests are shaped by cultural trends. Referring to the hysteria of the late nineteenth century and the depression or chronic fatigue syndrome of the late twentieth century, he emphasises the iatrogenic role of medical and mental health professions who he sees as 'creating' culturally appropriate symptoms.

Perhaps it is pertinent here to point out the importance of attending to symptoms as opposed to attempting to get rid of them. Indeed this is the true meaning of the term 'dia-gnosis' that is, seeing through the symptom. The term symptom itself comes from the Greek word *syn* meaning together, and *pitein* meaning to fall. A symptom then refers to two or more things that fall together. Meier (cited in Lockhart 1983, p. 64) suggests that it is body and psyche that fall together in symptoms.

As Lockhart argues: 'From the perspective of analytical psychology, a symptom not only expresses an underlying psychic process but also may represent a positive attempt by the unconscious to force the individual into a process of consciousness...' (1983, p. 9). He notes that to 'deprive an individual of his symptoms may be clothed in humanitarianism, but it may also deprive him of an opportunity to learn the meaning of his own life' (1983, p. 31).

When working with clients who bring physical symptoms with them, the temptation is often to avoid rather than observe what the body has to say about the client's current mental state (unless the counsellor is specifically trained in body based psychotherapies). As Thomas Moore (1992) suggests, we need to follow the will of the symptom and to engage in dialogue with the body. This is easier said than done, for the individual usually prefers to eradicate the body's anomalies before there is an opportunity to read them for their meaning. This is not surprising given that in contemporary society the body is viewed as a machine, which, if it breaks down, can be repaired with a mechanical substitute. In other words the intent to heal can get in the way of the healing (Freshwater, 1998).

The dichotomy that has and continues to exist between the psychological and the physical is unfortunate, and exemplifies Western dualistic thought. It is in fact a false dichotomy, one that favours a rather static either/or position, as opposed to a more fluid both/and position. Unfortunately this distinction has encouraged patients and many physicians to believe that the two are fundamentally different. But, as Kendall (1996,

p. 22) asks, 'what is the difference between psychiatric disorders like schizophrenia and obsessional disorder, and diseases of the brain like encephalitis and Parkinson's disease?' He answers his own question stating that there is fundamentally none:

> Psychiatric disorders tend to involve the patient's whole personality, his social behaviour and his ability to make rational responses to both incoming sensory information and internal cognitive assessments because they involve dysfunctions of the cerebral mechanisms responsible for perception, memory, cognition and mood. Their effects are therefore more global, pervasive and subtle than those of disorders of, for example, the gall bladder or the hip joint. (1996, p. 22)

This, he argues, is a difference of degree rather than a qualitative difference.

The link between physical and mental illness and social and economic status is well-documented (Broome, 1989; Townsend, Whitehead & Davidson, 1992). Lewis, Sullivan and Barraclough (1994) remind us that poorer people are more vulnerable to physical illnesses and disabilities, which in turn can lead to depression and anxiety. Further, poorer people are predisposed to mental illnesses, which in turn lowers immunity and is associated with health damaging behaviours, for example excessive smoking and drinking and malnutrition. And as Gomm opines:

> If you take any social group, or any neighbourhood with a high rate of premature death, or coronary heart disease...and so on, then the chances are that the group or neighbourhood will be a poor one, and that it will show high rates of suicides and depression and anxiety states and schizophrenia'. (1996, p. 112)

Thus there appears to exist a complex circular and cyclical relationship between social and economic conditions and physical illness and psychological stress.

In addition to the impact of stress, social and economic conditions, many other internal and external factors have been shown to affect the immune system and disease, including personality, psychiatric illness, coping style, positive attitudes, relaxation, hypnosis, meditation, guided imagery and humour. The aftermath of trauma often lives on in the form of somatic symptoms.

As counsellors it is important, therefore, to try to understand the nature of the bodily symptoms and why the trauma is somatised. Psychotherapeutic intervention can ameliorate such symptoms and help the client work towards well-being. Whilst most counsellors are not trained as body therapists they can perhaps work directly with the client's body–mind reality, their physical symptoms and the underlying unconscious dynamics.

3.2   A number of my clients are referred for anxiety/ panic related physical symptoms. What is the relationship between stress, anxiety and the body?

Anxiety is a normal human response to threatening and stressful situations. Stress and anxiety can be helpful, in that they can help us to avoid dangerous situations as well as motivate us to perform well. However, if such feelings go on for too long, or they are too strong, they can prevent us from doing the things we want to do and may eventually lead to physical illness. Counsellors may encounter clients experiencing anxiety and stress either as a primary presenting problem, or as secondary symptoms. Some medications can cause feelings of anxiety, as can some illnesses; for example, an overactive thyroid gland has similar symptoms to that of acute anxiety.

Anxiety, then, can be a symptom of both mental and physical illnesses and as such clients should always have physical symptoms investigated so as to rule out any underlying physical pathology. Anxiety is difficult to diagnose and is often confused with other mental illnesses, most significantly depression. People find it easier to admit to anxiety symptoms than those of depression (which still carries a stigma) and so present at their GP surgery with the physical symptoms associated with anxiety. To some extent the physical symptoms interact with the psychological symptoms (see Question 3.1). For example, a person experiencing anxiety might, when feeling their heart pounding, think they are having a heart attack. This can itself lead to anxiety further perpetuating the symptoms. Sudden unexpected surges of anxiety are called panic, often leading the individual to remove themselves from the situation they are in. The first documented experience of panic is listed as far back as the sixteenth century, when, in France, panic attacks were known as *terreur panique*. It was Freud in the 1880s who began calling them anxiety attacks, and it was not until the 1980s that the term panic attack found itself back in the medical and psychological domain, in the DSM-IV (see Question 2.1). Both anxiety and panic related symptoms can lead to the feelings of depression, not least as a direct result of the exhaustive nature of anxiety and panic themselves (Baker, 2003). Occasionally the anxiety becomes associated with a specific situation or object, leading to a phobic response, and it may be this that the patient presents with in the first instance.

Generalised anxiety disorder (GAD) (a condition of severe anxiety) is an intense long-lasting anxiety without any obvious cause and classically presents with physical symptoms. These physical symptoms include:

• pounding of the heart
• dry mouth

- sweating
- frequency of micturition
- dizziness
- feeling faint
- indigestion
- diarrhoea
- tinnitus
- muscle tension
- tension headaches
- shortness of breath
- nausea
- trembling or shaking.

Psychological indications include:

- feeling worried all the time
- feeling tired
- inability to concentrate
- feeling irritable
- sleeping badly.

Counsellors from different theoretical orientations respond to the presentation of symptoms in different ways. Whilst listing and labelling symptoms may give some a semblance of order (and therein control), what does this really tell us? It is perhaps a bit like quantum theory in that it depends on the observer: the doctor sees the physical (the particle), the counsellor or psychotherapist sees the underlying psychological (the wave). These are not mutually exclusive and together they form a wider and more complete picture. Finally, counsellors need to emphasise to the client that a certain degree of anxiety is normal and healthy, as anyone who has ever been in a car with someone who has no anxiety will understand!

3.3   Are there specific physical illnesses that impact on the client's mental health?

As already mentioned, physical ill health is known to be associated with mental ill health. Those people with chronic physical ill health have an increased risk of mental illness, in particular depression. Each individual responds to physical illness in a different and unique way, which is influenced by many other factors including socio-economic situation, support network, employment status and family position. However, it does seem that certain illnesses do have a greater impact on the client's mental health than others. Although most people are familiar with the idea that the psychological state influences physical conditions (indeed that it is hard to think of any condition that is not 'psychosomatically' influenced to some degree), counsellors need to be aware of the reverse polarity, that is, somatopsychic presentation, where medical conditions present primarily with psychological symptoms.

Flaherty, Channon and Davis (1989) itemise 11 different categories of medical conditions that may present with psychological symptoms. Neurological disorders, such as multiple sclerosis, Huntington's disease, Alzheimer's and epilepsy often have associated psychological symptoms. It is estimated that 30–50 per cent of epileptics have co-occuring psychiatric problems, with personality disorders or personality problems, anxiety, depression, withdrawal, destructive assaultive behaviour and obsessive–compulsive symptoms. Many patients with disorders of the endocrine system present with anxiety and depression, changes in eating behaviour and chronic fatigue. For example, hypothyroidism includes symptoms of loss of initiative, anorexia and fatigue.

It is more commonly known that cardiovascular disorders and pulmonary disorders are both associated with anxiety, as are gastrointestinal disorders. Particular attention has been paid to this category of illness where the initial presentation may revolve around symptoms of depression, loss of motivation and a sense of doom. These symptoms can predate the discovery of some diseases, such as pancreatic cancer, by years (Flaherty et al., 1989). Diseases of the blood, including anaemias, may present as depression and can include symptoms of anorexia, decreased libido, weakness and fatigue and anxiety, as can infectious diseases, metabolic and toxic disorders, and collagen vascular diseases, which can account for roughly 12 per cent of the medical causes of anxiety.

Specific physical illnesses that have an impact on the client's mental health can be divided into two broad categories. Those that cause emotional/mental symptoms as a direct result of hormonal or endocrine imbalances or degenerative changes (for example, an underactive or overactive thyroid gland and Alzheimer's) and those that cause a severe emotional reaction (such as a terminal cancer or multiple sclerosis). Any condition that is disabling, life threatening, painful and/or requiring imminent surgery is likely to impact on the client's mental health, particularly if they have little family or external support. Some drug treatments, such as steroids, affect the way the brain works and so may cause anxiety and depression directly.

It is not just the illness that impacts on the client's mental health; it can also be coping with the side effects of invasive treatment such as dialysis, or loss of control and increasing dependency on others. Other physical illnesses such as adult acne, psoriasis, alopecia and postural defects also have a great impact on self-image and the ability to form relationships, potentially leading to isolation, anxiety, depression and even suicide.

Nevertheless, since the majority of counsellors and psychotherapists are not medically qualified, physical symptoms should be checked out by a GP.

3.4   Is it true that certain biological and personality types are more prone to mental and physical illness?

Personality can be defined as a pattern of thought, feeling, motivation and behaviour that is expressed in day-to-day living. The theory of different personality types can be traced as far back as the ancient Greeks who identified four humours, namely the sanguine, the phlegmatic, the choleric and the melancholic. Although research indicates that some personality factors have a genetic component, for example, persistence, memory, sensitivity to stress, levels of aggression, levels of traditionalism, social closeness, positive and negative emotionality, shyness and sociability (Ludwig, 1999), this is not the full story. Other factors, such as environment, personal experience and cultural influences also have a determining effect. It is important, however, to distinguish between personality types and personality disorders. The DSM-IV defines 10 personality disorder types, and it is fair to say that these individuals would find it hard to maintain an adequate relationship with the counsellor. It is also fair to say that current research into personality types is helping us to better understand the connection between personality, psychopathology and illness and psychotherapy.

For example, the link between heart disease and the type A personality (characterised by hostility, time urgency, impatience, anxiety and excessive stress) has been the focus of many studies (see Martin, 1997 for an in-depth analysis of this subject). In one intervention study the effects of standard cardiac counselling alone were compared with a combination of cardiac counselling and counselling focused on reducing hostility and other components of type A behaviour. Compared with the control group, those that received the combined counselling showed reductions in type A behaviour and an almost 50 per cent reduction in subsequent heart attacks over the next five years.

In his book, *The Sickening Mind*, Paul Martin (1997) clearly defines the relationship between the mind and immunity, articulating what effect the immune system can have on the mind and vice versa. Posing many interesting and relevant questions, he contends that we are more likely to become physically ill in periods of excessive stress and when experiencing depression or anxiety. Interestingly he also links certain physical diseases with certain types of personality. Drawing on a number of authors he distinguishes between those diseases that, despite having no underlying organic pathology, manifest physical symptoms, and those in which psychological factors play a contributing role in the development of the illness.

Increasingly, behavioural scientists are finding relationships between certain personality traits and particular diseases. The emerging field of research concerned with the complex interrelationships between physical, psychological and emotional factors on the one hand and immunity and disease on the other is known as psychoneuroimmunology. Traditionally doctors and scientists have tended to view the immune system as an autonomous entity that operates independently of the mind. However, the importance of an individual's psychological state in determining their immune level was demonstrated over 30 years ago in a study surmising that immunosuppression could be psychologically conditioned (Ader & Cohen, 1975). Since then, writers and therapists have done much to progress the thesis that certain personality types are more prone to physical and mental illnesses, often linking this to genetic and/or hereditary factors.

3.5   Is depression a common response to physical illness?

As stated earlier in this chapter, the relationship between physical illness and depression is a complex and multifaceted one and depression often presents initially as one or more physical symptoms (Armstrong, 1997). In addition, depression often overlaps with other conditions and life events, making it difficult to identify. Many of the symptoms of physical illness, for example, are similar to those of depression, including poor appetite, lack of sleep, low energy or fatigue and low concentration. Further, those with painful and life-threatening physical illnesses are at increased risk of becoming depressed (Armstrong, 1997). In Question 2.8 the difference between endogenous and reactive depression was briefly examined. Reactive depression may occur as a result of a physical complaint, and it is not unusual for individuals with chronic debilitating illness to have concurrent depression (see also Question 3.3). Depression also presents in degrees of severity: most general practitioners assess whether the client has mild, moderate or severe depression prior to determining the best treatment plan (see also Question 2.9).

Katon et al. (1991) found that somatisation in primary care and in the community is frequently accompanied by symptoms of depression and anxiety. This connection is supported by multiple studies that also illuminate the high utilisation of health care facilities in this group. The authors suggest that 'both psychological and somatic symptoms may result from the same underlying physiological abnormalities...but it is also possible that depression and anxiety lower the threshold at which minor symptoms are perceived' (1991, p. 34). Perception may be increased or amplified, or illness related memories and a negative view of health might predominate.

Pain too can lead to a decrease in enjoyment of what were formerly pleasurable activities and lead to a withdrawal from social activity, which contributes to the despair. In addition, sleep may be impaired with similar results and a feedback loop begins that feeds the depression. Depression in the presence of physical illness should be treated in the same way as depression without physical illness.

3.6 I am working with a woman who has recently had a mastectomy. She claims that she still feels as if she has both breasts. Is this usual or is she developing hallucinations?

Hallucinations, defined as a person experiencing false sensory perceptions, are often seen as the archetypal symptom of mental illness. Brennan (2004, p. 366) notes that hallucinations do not emanate from the world around the individual, but are 'mental experiences that do not have the physical cause necessary for the experience to be a true sensory experience'. Hallucinations can originate from physical trauma to the brain, brain tumours, epilepsy and drug and alcohol disorders, as well as being indicative of a mental illness. Phantom limb pain, sometimes mistakenly labelled as a hallucination, does have a physical explanation located in the complex structures of the nervous system and can be described as both the psyche's and the body's attempt to heal the split between the episodic memory (the mastectomy) and the emotional memory (being whole). Such healing is often achieved through dreams. What we are perhaps looking at here is the client's desire to be a whole woman.

A counsellor can help by providing the opportunity to explore the feelings associated with this major surgery – feelings of hope and relief together with anger and confusion. The surgery may well have affected the patient's sexual feelings particularly if her breasts are important to sexual arousal for her or her partner. This may be accompanied by shame around the altered body appearance, and although the bruising and swelling will go down and the scar will fade, acceptance of the loss can be difficult.

It is likely that working with this client will involve a shifting focus moving from coping with the initial crisis and offering ego support to explorational psychotherapy. The loss of a breast challenges our fantasies of immortality and of control. Our bodies are not indestructible and we cannot control the world around or in us. Developmentally the ego is closely connected with the idea of an intact body, and if the body is threatened then our personhood is also under threat; that is, our self-worth will be undermined.

Cancer seems to strike irrationally and is often seen as an evil that unfairly throws our life into chaos. This can instigate overwhelming and intense emotional reactions that add to the feeling of being out of control. In addition, the loss of a breast, or any disfigurement, may trigger fears of abandonment, which are highlighted by the need, initially, to depend on others until physical healing occurs.

The counsellor might also explore with the client other fears about other aspects of her life – will the mastectomy interfere with, for example, her recreational activities? How will she cope with communal changing rooms or getting undressed when her children or husband are around? It is also usual to explore the meaning that the client attaches to her illness, as severe illness can precipitate issues around suffering and punishment and about responsibility. Too often a positive attitude is equated with a 'stiff upper lip' and many fear that expressing their feelings will worsen their illness, and that only a positive attitude will help. It can be quite reassuring to clients to hear the contrary view that feeling low and crying are appropriate and normal and they are not the same as 'giving up'. This may help them cope with the overwhelming tide of affect that often flows.

Often when dealing with people who have cancer their fears and anxieties are realistic, but addressing the unconscious meaning to the patient can be equally important. Working with the client to normalise the continued sensation of having two breasts, whilst also facilitating a relationship within which she can access and experience the emotions associated with such a traumatic disfigurement are important therapeutic tasks. Very often the therapist becomes especially important to the client and a positive transference develops arising from the need to return to a state of loving protection in the face of an existential threat. Counter-transference feelings may also be particularly strong, and supervision, as ever, will be important.

3.7   Is counselling suitable for clients who have both a terminal illness and a mental illness?

Having a history of mental illness does not mean that individuals are any less at risk from terminal illnesses; indeed, as discussed elsewhere in this chapter, many such patients have an increased risk of physical ill health. Mentally disturbed people are also susceptible to the feelings of shock, fear, anger, blame, guilt, denial, confusion and hurt that are often experienced by those who have to undergo intensive and invasive treatment. Knowledge of the patient's psychiatric history is usually helpful when assessing the client's suitability for counselling. Gaining an awareness of the wider picture can facilitate sensitivity to the differentiation of 'normal' reactions, such as an overwhelming flood of emotions, from the exacerbation of a known mental illness.

The counsellor can play an important role in encouraging a positive relationship with the patient's medical team, advocating and facilitating the asking of relevant questions and alleviating some of the (irrational) fears whilst helping to contain the reality of their distress. Counselling can, it could be argued, provide a safe space for anyone with a terminal illness to express how he or she is feeling and what they are thinking. Unravelling the emotions and worries and aiding an acceptance of the situation whilst offering support and care are important aspects of the terminally ill client's processing of their experience. In addition, there are often added pressures of finance, finding care, what to say to children, concern for other members of the family and so on, that can also benefit from being shared with a person external to the situation.

As with any counselling and psychotherapy practice, the counsellor is challenged to look closely at themselves and assess their own capabilities in dealing with existential issues, as well as their own beliefs and values. The euthanasia debate, which it seems is and will continue to be a consistently contentious issue, has raised the profile of some of the difficult decisions with which individuals are faced. One debate found the *Right to Life* group arguing that counselling is the only way of properly dealing with terminal illness (BBC News, 23 September 2003). Their concern was that because depression often accompanies terminal illness, a decision to end life is not taken while of sound mind. Suicidal ideation is often an indicator of a major depressive episode. However, in the case of terminal illness the boundaries are blurred.

Counselling and psychotherapy are just one part of a network of support available to the patient and their family and as such the counsellor working in this field needs to be aware of supporting agencies and specialist services, thus enabling a multifaceted and multidisciplinary approach to the care (see also Chapter 6).

3.8 A young male client has recently been referred to me for his self-harming behaviour. Is counselling a suitable treatment?

Self-harm is a complex phenomenon, for which there is a whole range of possible causes. It is viewed as diversely as ritual 'tribal' behaviour, as well as evidence of 'psychological stress and anxiety'. It has also been carried out in cases of severe disorder of thoughts, feelings or behaviour, as in episodes of psychosis. In most industrialised (Western) societies, it is regarded as being outside the range of 'normal acceptable' behaviour associated with mental stability and well-being, and has frequently been cited as evidence of 'mental health' problems. In mental health settings such behaviours are frequently viewed as evidence of manipulative tendencies, or as a visual representation of psychological distress.

The real number of persons engaging in any form of deliberate self-harm is generally unknown, but is probably much more widespread than the available figures would suggest. Self-harm is a broad term for acts, deliberate or not, which cause personal harm. This can range from not taking care of one's own emotional or physical needs, smoking or drinking to excess, or becoming repeatedly involved in abusive relationships, through to more direct acts of self-injury. These include cutting, scratching, burning, self-hitting, hair pulling, bruising or bone breaking and interfering with wound healing, but exclude acts with a conscious suicidal intent or that are associated with sexual arousal. However, any attempt to achieve a consensus of what constitutes an act of self-harm should be viewed with caution not least because it is a behaviour complicated by cultural interpretations. In some societies, deliberate acts of self-mutilation may be considered as evidence of mental instability or personal torment, whereas in other communities similar actions are frequently regarded as the social norm; in fact in some populations such activities may even be positively encouraged as in the case of tribal initiations or religious acts of self-mortification.

It is interesting to note that in the 1990s, Mosby's (Anderson, 1994) dictionary defined those groups at risk of self-harm as including clients with borderline personality disorder (especially females aged 16–25 years), clients in a psychotic state (frequently males in young adulthood), emotionally disturbed or battered children, mentally retarded and autistic children, clients with a history of self-injury, and clients with a history of physical, emotional or sexual abuse. It is now estimated that 4–5 people per 1000 of the population self-harm, and whilst some studies suggest that the rates are 2–3 times higher in women than in men, it has also been argued that the gaps in sex-specific rates are closing, at least within the United Kingdom (Department of Health, 2002b; NHS Centre for Reviews and Dissemination, 1998).

It is important as hinted above to observe the distinction between self-harm and suicide. Self-harm, paradoxically, is a means of survival, not destruction. In other words it can provide a way of coping with overwhelming emotions, feelings of helplessness and of being powerless. There is often an absence of pain during the act of self-injury rather like the absence of sensation when the body's own defence system numbs the emotions at times of trauma. This dissociation often occurs during abuse and many people who self-harm have been sexually abused (see Walker, 2003, pp. 61–64), although not all those who have been abused self-injure and not all those who self-harm have been abused.

Whilst suicide is more prevalent in males, deliberate self-harm occurs more frequently among females, although as mentioned there has been a recent steep rise in its occurrence among young men. (Data from the Office of National Statistics show that as many as one in 10 teenagers deliberately self-harm and that rates of deliberate self-harm among young men and boys have almost doubled since the 1980s.) Unfortunately individuals who self-harm are often judged adversely by those who treat them in medical settings and stories abound of those who have self-harmed reporting that they were sutured without anaesthetic, or coldly dismissed into the world without assurance of any support network.

Clinical psychologists may offer behavioural techniques to help; this may include keeping a diary to identify 'triggering' behaviour and finding other channels through which to release the feelings. This is only one approach to managing the behaviour, however, and does not necessarily address the underlying causes. The Department of Health (2002a, 2002b) identified problem-solving therapies, dialectical therapies (DBT) and assertive outreach as providing some relief in reducing episodes of self-harm. Therapeutic approaches that enabled women to address underlying causes and to find more positive coping strategies were also recommended.

Counselling can offer such patients the chance to talk through feelings in confidence without being judged. Nevertheless, it should be noted that working with clients with self-harming behaviours can be very distressing and frustrating for counsellors. As always the importance of good supervision cannot be overstated. Trust is a very important issue along with acceptance of self-harming behaviours, although this involves not an encouragement to continue but recognition that self-harm is an attempt to survive. Once accepted that self-harm or self-injury is acceptable to talk about, there may be an opportunity to find an alternative way of dealing with emotional pain, at which point the possibility of long-term psychotherapy might be considered.

3.9 Is it true that substance misuse can lead to mental illness?

Some drugs can induce psychosis and this may often be confused with schizophrenia or other acute mental illness. In fact acute mental illness caused by cannabis ingestion is now a common cause of hospital admission (see, for example, www.globalchange.com). Different drugs produce different effects and it is hard to separate these, especially when the combined effect manifests like an acute psychotic state indistinguishable from many other mental disorders. The diagnosis may only become clear when the person who is unwell reveals the full history of what they have tried and when. The difference from other diagnoses is that drug-induced hallucinations, delusions and distortions disappear with abstinence from drugs.

A diagnosis of a severe mental health problem *together with* a substance misuse (drug or alcohol) problem is called 'dual diagnosis'. It is not a simple situation as the effects of the substance misuse can be mistaken for a mental health problem because the symptomatic presentation can be similar. It can also be difficult to tell which problem came first; sometimes a mental health problem can be caused by, or made worse by, substance misuse. In other situations the substance misuse might be a result of a mental health problem, as people with mental health problems are often very vulnerable members of society and are lured into the 'sales pitch' that claims drugs or alcohol will block feelings of isolation, loneliness, boredom or depression and improve confidence and self-esteem.

Often without much social or emotional support such an elixir is hard to resist. The truth is, however, that substance misuse can have a dramatic negative impact on psychotic disorders and can exacerbate symptoms. Some substances, particularly alcohol, cannabinoids, hallucinogens and stimulants can also produce psychotic symptoms directly, without the presence of mental illness. However, according to some writers, although these substances may trigger psychotic disorders amongst people with a predisposition, the existence of any stronger causal relationship remains controversial (Stimpson, 1999). Researchers in the United Kingdom disagree, and more recently findings from a study led by Ilana Crome (Crome, Ghodse, Gilvarry & McArdle, 2004) indicate that the number of people who are both mentally ill and abusing drugs had increased by 60 per cent over five years. The findings also reinforce earlier evidence of the link between psychotic symptoms, schizophrenia and depression and the use of illegal drugs, specifically cannabis.

Some theoretical models place more reliance on 'vulnerability' factors than on actual consumption of drugs. For example, the Twelve-Step model suggests that certain users of drugs are particularly prone to experience difficulty, rather than viewing drugs *per se* as responsible for the development of problems. Vulnerable individuals are seen as manifesting a pre-existing and enduring tendency to develop problems whenever drugs are used. (For a comprehensive review of the relationship between addiction, drug and alcohol use and mental illness the reader is referred to the companion text on *Addiction*, edited by Reading and Jacobs, 2003.)

Knowing that a client has a drug related mental disorder the counsellor might perhaps be more sensitive to signs of difficulty with engaging the client in a therapeutic relationship. Drug induced mental illness can involve violent behaviour and the safety of self and client is of course very important. Patients with a dual diagnosis tend to have complex long-term needs and probably require long-term support and counselling.

CHAPTER 4

Socio-political influences: The social construction of mental illness[1]

4.1 How is mental illness currently being conceptualised within the social and political context?

Spending some time reflecting on the social construction of mental illness may be seen as a merely academic exercise of little practical value, indulgent even in the face of real psychological and emotional distress. Furthermore, such theorising may be seen as leading to a paralysis of professionals and their helpful intervention in the lives of individual sufferers. However, by highlighting the nature of the concept of mental illness, we strip it of its common-sense veneer and trouble its taken-for-granted meaning in order to surface alternative, competing and maybe less comfortable explanations of distress and 'madness'. It may be tempting to look on modern theories of mental illness as real and concrete, and diagnostic categories as valid and reliable, both the results of the evidence produced in carefully designed scientific research programmes. However, as Ion and Beer (2003) remind us, an understanding of the history of psychiatry and mental health care can help us gain insights into how modern approaches and treatments have been influenced as much by socio-political factors and power relationships as by scientific studies. Moreover, sociologists have added a considerable amount to the concepts of mental disorder and to the debate surrounding diagnostic categories and the practice of mental health professionals, including counsellors and psychotherapists, which in itself deserves attention (Busfield, 2001).

As well as individual and life course differences, there are structural differences in the distribution of psychological and emotional distress and

---

[1] This chapter was written by Dawn Freshwater with contributions from Sabi Redwood.

the way it is experienced between men and women, and between white and black people, for example. There is also evidence that whether people are men or women, white or black, affects the way they are treated in the mental health system (Barnes & Bowl, 2001). So while it is necessary to understand the way in which psychological and emotional distress affects individuals and those immediately around them, it cannot be seen in isolation from the responses they receive from mental health professionals and the messages they get about mental illness through their environment. These reactions in turn reflect the dominant discourses about how mental illness is defined and negotiated (Barnes & Bowl, 2001; Freshwater, 2003). The definitions of mental illness do not have a reality independent of the society in which they occur, but they are spoken into existence according to the values and beliefs that shape the discourse about what is 'normal' and 'abnormal', or 'natural' and 'unnatural'. Therefore, in a society where reason and rationality are highly prized, the loss of reason, or madness, presents a profound threat. The work of Emile Durkheim (1964) is insightful in this area and in particular his understanding of the rules and standards that define what is pathological and how these reinforce the norms and values of society.

Constructionist dialogues replace traditional interests in objectivity and truth with concerns related to discourse and practice (Gergen & Gergen 2003). Such dialogues are made possible by the idea that we live in a world of meaning making and language, which are used to 'do things'. In other words, meaning and language are inextricably linked to our actions and our practice. Professionals in mental health care try to explain, predict and control mental illness through their privileged knowledge. Their expertise lies in making the diagnosis, in prescribing treatment and in reorienting patients to live in the 'real' world in order to restore them to 'normal' functioning. However, notions about what is 'real' and 'normal' in a society are not determined through the application of a universal standard, but are social constructions driven by relations of power and control.

To illustrate this point, Fernando (2002) suggests that the social construction of mental illness is brought into sharp relief by the political abuses of psychiatry in the former Soviet Union and in the decision of the American Psychiatric Association in 1973 that homosexuality should no longer be seen as a pathological condition. What these actions show is that rather than mental illness being defined against some absolute yardstick, the process of labelling is generated through and by powerful societal institutions that have the authority to both constrain and liberate individuals. The social constructionist perspective challenges the notion of mental illness as the result of biological, genetic and psychological malfunctioning. Rather, it sees psychiatric pathology as the labels given to the damaging effect of disadvantage and discrimination, such as racism or homophobia, on the identity of individuals. These in turn are likely to lead to experiences of alienation arising from a socio-political system that denies those individuals the opportunity to express themselves, to be heard and understood, or to live in a particular way. Williams (1999) suggests that behaviours defined as symptoms or disordered can be understood as creative responses to difficult personal and social histories, rooted in a person's oppression.

4.2 Are there cultural differences in the way that mental illness is assessed, treated and understood?

In order to answer this question fully, it is first of all important to understand the concept of culture and its relationship to race and ethnicity. The concept of culture has been much defined, and any definition is grounded in a particular time, place and perspective. Hofstede (2001), for example, offers what Kluckhohn calls a 'well known, anthropological consensus definition of culture: Culture consists in patterned ways of thinking, feeling and reacting, acquired and transmitted mainly through symbols, consisting the distinctive achievements of human groups, including their embodiments in artefacts; the essential core of culture consists of traditional ... ideas and especially their attached values' (Kluckhohn, 1951 cited in Hofstede, 2001, p. 9). Although a useful starting point for thinking about culture, this definition runs the risk of viewing cultures as distinct, homogeneous and static. Categorisations that lump people together have become questionable because they give rise to unhelpful generalisation and stereotypes which deny difference between individuals in cultures. We have also become suspicious of attempts to offer definitions that refer to a meaning which appears uncontested, stable and apolitical.

Exploring culture from a postmodern position may help to open up new perspectives and to offer alternative ways to think about culture and mental illness. The following definition by Helman (2000, p. 2) moves towards a more helpful understanding of culture as shaping the conceptual structures that determine the interpretations of experience and how reality is both lived and constructed by people: 'culture is a set of guidelines (both explicit and implicit) that individuals inherit as members of a particular society, and that tell them how to view the world, how to experience it emotionally, and how to behave in it in relation to other people, to supernatural forces or gods, and to the natural environment. It also provides them with a way of transmitting these guidelines to the next generation – by the use of symbols, language, art and ritual'.

The term culture has been confused with 'race' in both popular and professional discourse. Fernando (2002, p. 36) suggests that this is 'mainly because people who are seen as racially different are conceptualised as having different cultures, and the term culture is used to conceal racism'. The term 'ethnicity' has been used to replace both race and culture as a basis for defining a group of people who feel themselves different in relation to other groups. Although the term has both racial and cultural connotations, its main purpose is to convey a sense of belonging together. The notion that persons who share physical characteristics, such as skin colour, belong to a 'race' that is genetically and biologically determined persists in influencing popular and professional opinion. This is despite genetic studies which have strengthened the view that racial difference on the basis of traditional criteria such as skin colour and physical appearance as an indication of biological difference is indefensible. Pearce, Foliaki, Sporle and Cunningham (2004) suggest that there are few genetic differences between 'races' as far as genes that affect health are concerned, and conclude that ethnic differences in health are more likely to be a result of historical, cultural and socio-economic factors, which in turn influence lifestyle and access to health care. However, despite the notion of race and racial categorisation on the basis of genetics being debunked as a biological myth, or at least as misleading, it nevertheless continues to be a social reality for many (Fernando, 2002).

The notion of 'mental health' and 'mental illness' derive from a particular tradition of medical research and practice that cannot provide a neutral stance from which to analyse or represent the way other cultures conceptualise disorders of behaving, feeling and mental functioning. Even the distinction between the body and the mind, and thereby between physical and mental illness, is in itself a social and cultural construction, as mentioned in Chapter 3 (Fernando, 2002). The notion of mental illness is rooted in Western thinking, attitudes and beliefs that have a limited perspective, yet claim to have universal relevance. The separation of body and mind is not evident in other cultures. However, as a result of the power of Western 'scientific' thinking, as well as Western political and economic global domination, and often racist discourses, other cultures' belief systems are considered to be inferior. This has led to an ignorance of alternative conceptualisations of spirituality, religion, community and family, as well as of distress and coping.

There are a number of resources that explore the role of spirituality, holistic thinking and non-Western explanatory models of illness and traditions of medicine (see, for example, Fernando, 2002). Although it may be impossible for counsellors and therapists to gain a profound knowledge of all cultural conceptualisations of health, well-being and ill health, some familiarity with some of the constructions may be useful in order to develop a sensitivity to clients' differences in cultural understandings of psychological and emotional distress. For example, research by Warner (1996) highlighted that the Shona of Zimbabwe believe visual and auditory hallucinations not only are real, but are also sent by spirits. Moreover, the fact that individuals remain integrated within their community group, and that the 'illness' has a culturally relevant content and context, means that the majority of acute psychoses are short lived and one-off episodes. Some cultures emphasise the nature of predetermination or divine intervention in response to mental distress; others focus on familial responsibility or fate and karmic consequence. Symptoms may be viewed as bad luck, misfortune, or the result of karmic payback for some past wrongdoing. Health may be viewed as a harmony between complementary energies. The important message for counsellors is that what may be considered 'mad' in one culture may not be in another (Wilson & Francis 1997).

One of the cultural assumptions of Western psychiatry is that its theories about mental health and illness apply globally and that psychiatric diagnoses such as depression or psychosis are universally valid. Similarly, it is taken for granted that the concept of identity as a fixed and stable entity and a unique and individualistic quality holds true across cultures. Although cultural differences within the traditional Western psychiatric discourse are viewed as giving structure and meaning to the experience of mental distress (Burr, 2002; Yen & Wilbraham, 2003), they are relegated to mere embellishments on the underlying reality of psychiatric abnormality. For example, the fact that an individual may hear voices is given greater diagnostic importance than what the voices are actually saying. The content is seen to be culturally constituted, whereas the very presence of voices signals that psychiatric pathology is present (Yen & Wilbraham, 2003). Kleinman (1980, 1988) challenges this view. Rather than conceiving of symptoms and pathology as universal, he proposes that the course of an illness is shaped by the local world of the person suffering distress. Therefore, the description of a certain experience as 'mental illness' and the course of treatment developed in one cultural group may not be applicable to people who share a different set of cultural beliefs about illness and treatment. In an integrative view of health the political, the economic, the moral and the medical are inextricably linked (James & Prilleltensky, 2002; Kleinman & Becker, 1998).

This may have implications for counsellors and therapists who may value, for example, notions of equality as a pre-requisite for practice. These values may come into conflict with other cultural notions in which relationships are seen to function and to be maintained on a hierarchical basis that includes elders and extended family networks. Similarly, the idea of the counsellor or therapist as companion on a journey could come into conflict with cultures where the spiritual guru is the perceived authority. It is also important to recognise that mental health interventions that promote the recognition of the importance of the individual, individuation, personal responsibility and insight may not be appropriate or relevant for some cultures and belief systems. In Western cultures the 'self' is viewed as independent and autonomous and the emphasis is on the freedom of the individual. This contrasts with many non-Western cultures where the model is one of interdependence and mutuality (for example Native Americans emphasise 'we-ness' not 'me-ness').

4.3   Is it true that African-Caribbean men are more likely to develop/be diagnosed with schizophrenia?

The theory and practice of psychiatry and psychology are grounded in Western views, attitudes and beliefs that define mental illness as expressions of abnormalities of mental functioning (see Question 2.1). They produce ethnocentric discourses that are assumed to have universal applicability and relevance. This assumption has led to a racial bias in the practice of psychiatry, which in turn has resulted in differences in diagnostic patterns, management and outcomes of mental illness across ethnic groups (Bhui, McKenzie & Gill, 2004; Bracken & Thomas, 2001; Burman, Gowrisunkur & Walker, 2003; Desai, 2003). For example, rates of suicide are higher among some South Asian women and young people of African-Caribbean origin (Raleigh, 1996). Schizophrenia in African-Caribbean men is another example of racial difference in diagnostic patterns.

Despite a recent report that proposes that African-Caribbean people do *not* have significantly higher rates of psychotic illness than other population groups (Joint Health Surveys Unit of the National Centre for Social Research, and the University College London for the Department of Health 2000), there is evidence to suggest that they are more likely than white people to be diagnosed with a mental health problem. They are also more likely to be diagnosed and admitted to hospital for schizophrenia, and to be admitted to secure psychiatric units (Bhui etal., 2003; Raleigh, 1996). More African-Caribbean people than their white counterparts access psychiatric services via adversarial routes through the police under a section of the Mental Health Act and are given medication. Fewer are offered therapies such as psychotherapy (Mental Health Foundation, 2003). The reasons why African-Caribbean people have a more coercive relationship with mental health services remain unclear despite over 20 years of research (Morgan, Mallett, Hutchinson & Leff 2004). A range of explanations has been put forward to account for the high numbers of African-Caribbean and other 'minority groups' in the mental health system, including biomedical and genetic explanations, transcultural explanations and others pertaining to migration and culture conflict (Desai, 2003).

The Mental Health Foundation (2003) and the Sainsbury Centre for Mental Health (Keating, Robertson, McCulloch & Francis 2002) propose that a contributing factor may be that African-Caribbean people are reluctant to access mental health care through primary care settings because they fear the stigma of mental illness; they perceive psychiatry to be intrusive and mental health professionals as engaging in forms of discrimination and social control. As a result of their reluctance to seek help in the early stages of illness their distress worsens. Subsequently, many come to the attention of the police and are compulsorily admitted to hospital. The downward cycle often continues when African-Caribbean people are in the mental health system since those with a diagnosis of severe mental illness such as schizophrenia often disengage from the system, leading to social exclusion and a deterioration in mental health (Keating et al., 2002; Rose, Ford, Lindley, Gawith & the KCW Mental Health Monitoring Users' Group, 1998; Sainsbury Centre for Mental Health, 1998). Furthermore, this cycle is said to be fuelled by prejudice, misunderstanding, misconceptions, and individual and institutional racism (National Institute for Mental Health in England, 2003). Keating et al. (2002, p. 8) assert that 'stereotypical views of Black people, racism, cultural ignorance, and stigma and anxiety associated with mental illness often combine to undermine the way the health services assess and respond to the need of Black and African Caribbean communities'. Fernando (2002) seeks to explain the greater likelihood of African-Caribbean people, especially men, to be diagnosed as schizophrenic, and the greater use of coercion in interventions as products of the ethnocentricity and racism of Western society and psychiatry. This constructs black people as 'other' and therefore problematic, and black schizophrenic men as aggressive, violent and dangerous (Morgan et al., 2004). African-Caribbean people's suspicion of mental health services are not alleviated by the death of black psychiatric patients like David Bennett who stopped breathing after being restrained by six members of staff in a regional secure unit in October 1998.

The illness of schizophrenia has been described as 'a particular way of adapting both physically and socially to what is felt to be a deeply hostile environment' (Delor & Hubert, 2000, p. 1566). Given the social and political experiences of disempowerment, exclusion and racism that many African-Caribbean people in British society experience, schizophrenia has been understood as an adaptation to the risk of alienation, even if it takes the extreme shape of the dislocation and disintegration of the individual's identity. Other explanations identify genetic differences as a possible causative factor in the higher incidence of serious mental illness in African-Caribbean people. However, rates of schizophrenia in Trinidad and Barbados, which were studied and compared with those in London, were found to be lower, suggesting that there is no increased genetic vulnerability to schizophrenia in African-Caribbean populations (Bhugra et al., 2000). The same study also found that the incidence of schizophrenia was higher among second generation African-Caribbean people than in those who originally migrated to the United Kingdom. A study by Boydell et al. (2001) identifies social and environmental factors such as stress caused by racism, unemployment, poor housing and a lack of cultural identity as possible contributive factors. It may be therefore that therapists and counsellors need to pay much more attention to these factors than is commonly the case.

4.4   How can counsellors permit diversity and difference whilst simultaneously maintaining the clients' (and others') safety?

The way the 'other' is perceived in the dominant culture, as for example Western European or North American culture, is an important consideration when thinking about diversity and safety in counselling and psychotherapy practice. Definitions of 'other-ness' or difference in professional and public discourse are, like the discourse on mental illness, socially constructed. They are linked to issues of power and privilege even though they may masquerade under the mantle of scientifically-based truth, reason and objectivity. The 'other' is defined as 'other' insofar as it is different from what is constructed to be the norm. The norm in terms of social power in Western European and American society is usually defined as white, male, able-bodied, rational, English speaking, middle class and heterosexual. This positions black women, gay men or wheelchair users, for example, as bearers of difference because they deviate from that norm. Discourses may render the 'other' invisible, as for example lesbian women whose relationships are ignored or trivialised; or they may vilify groups like African-Caribbean men as violent and irrational and in need of containment and control; or they may prescribe attempts to rehabilitate cultural difference to better resemble the norm by attributing blame for mental illness to specific cultural practices as causing pathology. The role of women in some communities, for example, has been identified as leading to a low rate of reported depression and a high rate of suicide in South Asian women (Burr, 2002). Furthermore, these discourses attain a status of common sense, as for example the myth that South Asian families 'look after their own', that African-Caribbean people require larger doses of medication on the basis of their different physiology, or that African-Caribbean and South Asian people's linguistic abilities mean that they cannot benefit from 'talking therapies' (Desai, 2003). Such assertions can lead to unhelpful gener-alisations that deny individuals within cultural groups their uniqueness, and to labelling and stereotypes that generate potential for misunderstandings, inappropriate diagnoses and treatments, alienation and exclusion.

Health, social and welfare policy as well as human rights legislation are powerful drivers in addressing racism, sexism and homophobia and in declaring discrimination on the basis of ethnic background, gender or sexual orientation unacceptable. Furthermore, all current statutory services claim to be multicultural and aim towards an inclusive model of practice. However, Burman et al. (2003, p. 64) warn that subscription to 'intercultural and multicultural approaches can too easily turn the complexities of multiple and intersecting identities into separable variables that ignore the diversities of lived experience'. In other words, rather than attending to the lived experience of the individual, unhelpful generalisations and categorisations may reduce services' ability to sensitively respond to clients' stories and their distress. Indeed, although policy and mission statements may espouse anti-oppressive and anti-discriminatory practice, these aspirations are usually tested by the way individual incidents of alleged abuse are investigated and managed by the organisation.

The prevalence of stereotyping in our society indicates that the function of 'labelling' is to situate ourselves within society and as such is a normal and necessary part of being human. However, to believe this labelling to be globally true leads to stereotyping and to act on this results in prejudice, which in turn leads to oppressive behaviour. We are all affected by our personal stereotypes, consciously or unconsciously, when we meet other people; but the reality is that concepts of culture and race are not so clearly defined as we would maybe like to think: in addition to the counsellor's perception, each individual client has their own perception of how they fit into 'definitions' and this perception will change within each situation and over time. When this labelling is unconscious (or conscious but unchallenged) stereotypes can influence the diagnosis and treatment that people receive, and this leads to poor access or inappropriate treatment resulting in under- or over-diagnosis based on, for example, racist, geographical, socio-economic or gendered assumptions.

Any labelling of difference that marginalises or excludes contributes to feelings of isolation, fear, low self-esteem and anger, often resulting in depression in the face of the hopelessness that comes from the inability to control external forces. Labelling can also act as a barrier to accessing mental health services either through direct or perceived discrimination or through indirect discrimination such as difficulties with language. The underlying ethos of counselling is that all people are equal and that positive regard is offered unconditionally, unaffected by the diversity of skin colour, language, gender, religion, socio-economic status, disability or any other 'difference'.

It is argued here that a person cannot be separated from their context. This of course includes the counsellor and counselling too. To focus solely on Western ideology can result in unnecessary pathologising of behaviour that can be explained and treated in other ways. In other words, counselling and psychotherapy are also culturally bound, and are not necessarily viewed by all as benevolent and supportive. Furthermore, counselling uses a specific (and often exclusive) language that does not easily transcend culture. The recognition of language differences and the importance of language to identify needs also requires some consideration (Jung, 1987).

The acceptance of other cultures with their differing systems of thoughts, beliefs and practices challenges our empathic abilities as counsellors and reaffirms the importance of unconditional positive regard. If counselling is really about therapeutic relationships and the interface between the inner world of the client and the outer world of the contextual culture, then knowledge of this culture is essential. Working more deeply with the unconscious, which enfolds both inner and outer worlds, further emphasises the necessity of cross-cultural knowledge. Understanding and accepting diversity and difference in the assessment and understanding of mental illness does not jeopardise the majority neither does it preclude care for the individual. On the contrary, by working with cultural understanding we should be able to provide *better* care for all.

4.5 Some feminist counsellors believe that women are more likely to be diagnosed with mental illness than men are. Is there any evidence for this?

Women have been shut up in asylums from as far back as the sixteenth century, for anything from pregnancy to prostitution to witchcraft. More recently, Chesler (1996) argued that more women are seeking psychiatric help and being hospitalised than at any other time in history. Whilst general population studies suggest that the overall prevalence of mental illness is not significantly different between men and women, there are gender differences both within the specific disorders diagnosed and the way in which mental illness is presented. According to the National Institute for Mental Health in England in their document *Women's Mental Health: Into the Mainstream* (Department of Health, 2002b), anxiety, depression and eating disorders are up to two times more common in women, with substance misuse and antisocial personality disorders being more common in men. Schizophrenia and bipolar affective disorder do not show clear gender differences, although these demographics are obviously as dynamic as society is. It is only recently that figures regarding the high incidence of self-harm and eating disorders amongst young men has come to light, with suicide being the second most common cause of death among men in the 16–25-year-old age group. Currently mental health care does not adequately reflect and respond to such gender differences, with women's needs at times being poorly met (Department of Health, 2002b).

There is much speculation as to the reasons for women presenting with specific disorders as indicated. In addition to the usual factors influencing mental health status, such as financial, employment, physical and familial factors, women's mental health is affected by 'child sexual abuse, domestic violence, sexual violence and rape' (Department of Health, 2002b, p. 12; see also Walker, 2003). The low societal value still placed on a woman's role in the home, with the concomitant subordination of her needs to those of her children, is a potential negative influence on self-worth and may well contribute to mental ill health. This together with the social isolation often experienced by women (frequently linked to poverty) due to single parent-hood, lack of mobility (particularly in rural areas), feeling tied to the home because of children or elderly parents, lack of transport or fear of attack if they go out alone, all increases the risk of mental ill health and particularly of depression.

Depression is also linked to hormonal changes in adolescence, after childbirth (post-natal depression) or during the menopause. This, coupled with the fact women have a higher level of help-seeking behaviour, means that women are more likely to present and subsequently be diagnosed with mental illness (in particular depression) than men. Men, it is argued, are more likely to indulge their impulse in socially deviant ways, such as rape, burglary and other criminal activities and alcohol abuse. Chesler (1996) contests that depression rather than aggression is the female reaction to disappointment and loss. Hence it is important to separate out the actual prevalence of mental illness across gender from the presentation and diagnosis. It would seem that women are more likely to be diagnosed with mental illness because of their willingness to seek help. This does not mean, however, that women are not wrongly diagnosed or labelled as mentally ill.

In spite of government strategies purporting to offer psychological therapies routinely to all patients, women say that medication is often the only option on offer, although their desire is for greater access to 'talking treatments' (Department of Health, 2002b, p. 25). The interplay between gender, culture and ethnicity is of particular concern especially in the increased prevalence of suicide, self-harm and eating disorders in Asian adolescent girls; of post-traumatic stress disorder (PTSD) in women refugees who have suffered rape alongside displacement, loss of home and families; and with elderly women who have a higher life expectancy and may find themselves living alone with inadequate financial support.

In short, whilst it may be the case that more women admit to experiencing mental ill health, and even being diagnosed with mental illness, they continue to be under-represented in specialist health services, remain a minority group and are often overlooked when it comes to more clearly differentiated clinical diagnoses. Despite the complexity of both presentation and character of mental illness in women, Ryrie and Norman (2004, p. 12), referring to a wealth of literature, suggest that the lower number of women in specialist mental health services is a 'marker for the diagnostic practices and expectations of practitioners, which are different for men than for women'.

4.6   I work in a young offender's unit as a counsellor. I have noticed an increase in the amount of suicide attempts in this age group over the past two years. Are young people becoming susceptible to mental instability?

Completed suicide is relatively rare before puberty. However, its incidence increases with the onset of adolescence and, in particular it seems, in males across the USA (Basu, 2004; Shaffer, Gould & Fisher, 1996). It does appear from both traditional research evidence and wider media coverage that young adults are experiencing a high level of mental vulnerability in contemporary society, and there are grave concerns relating to the amount of antidepressant medication being prescribed to this age group. High proportions of suicides now occur in young adult males, with suicide being the commonest form of death in men under 35 years. In the United Kingdom the Samaritans report that every week 12 young men commit suicide, representing an increase of 60 per cent in the 15–24 year age group. Suicide is the ninth leading cause of all deaths in the USA and, tragically, is the third leading cause of death among young people aged 15–24. In Australia, there is currently a growing problem of suicide in young white adults, although there has been a problem with suicide in the indigenous population for many years. The National Institute for Mental Health in England (NIMHE) acknowledges the need to establish effective systems to encourage young men to access mental health services. A review of the available literature reveals that there is very little evidence of effective approaches to promoting mental health in this population. NIMHE intends to develop a mental health promotion project aimed at encouraging young men to seek help before their problems become critical. The increase in mental distress and the subsequent rise in the suicide rate in children and adolescents has prompted the inclusion of a comprehensive package of care recommendations within the Department of Health's (2004) National Service Framework for Children, Adolescents and Maternity Services.

Given that factors identified in the background of young people who attempt suicide include disruptive home circumstances and higher rates of psychiatric disorder in other family members, including addictive behaviours, it is highly likely that a higher percentage of people admitted to young offender institutions (YOI) will experience suicidal ideation. It is well documented that many young males within YOIs do attempt suicide and a significant number are unfortunately successful. Counsellors working within young offender institutions no doubt see the sharp end of this work and are faced with some very distressed and disturbed human beings. In addition, they work in environments that test their professional resilience (Freshwater, Walsh & Storey, 2001, 2002) and require high-quality restorative and normalising supervision. (For a detailed and extended review of supervision in counselling and therapy, readers are pointed to the companion volume in this series by Walker & Jacobs, 2004).

4.7 Is there any point in using counselling techniques with a client who has Alzheimer's disease?

Alzheimer's disease is thought to be the most common cause of dementia in older people, typified by a severe loss of memory and inability to recall even the most simplest of facts. Alzheimer's and dementia lead to behavioural problems such as agitation and mental health problems such as depression. Alzheimer's is a progressive disease that has a profound effect on both the patient and the family members. However, as the Alzheimer's Disease International (ADI) reminds us, an individual with the disease continues to be a person of worth and dignity, deserving the same respect as any other human being.

In recent years pharmaceutical interventions for Alzheimer's have grown considerably and GPs have been tasked with early diagnosis and treatment to enable the full range of positive outcomes to be available, including such treatments as memory rehabilitation, behaviour modification, reality orientation, reminiscence, art therapy and music therapy. Counselling and psychotherapy have not always been focused on the older person and, as many counsellors know, older people have not always held counselling in high regard. However, more recently there has been a growing body of evidence supporting the use of psychological therapies with older people (Keady & Ashton, 2004). Whilst much of the evidence concentrates on cognitive–behavioural therapies (CBT), Keady and Ashton (2004, p. 571) observe that there is an increasing person-centred and psychodynamic movement (see, for example, Jones and Miesen, 1991). They say that 'the need for self expression has recently culminated in people with dementia putting forward their needs for self-advocacy on an international platform' (Friedell & Bryden, 2002). Perhaps then, there is a purpose in counselling for people with dementia. Whether or not the 'talking' makes sense is not necessarily the essence of the so-called 'talking cure'.

Jung insisted that the *content* of psychotic talk was not only meaningful but also contained messages concerning psychic processes. He likened such talk to archaeological discoveries of ancient and unknown languages. Our task, as counsellors is not to deprecate such talk as plain crazy, but, as Lockhart (1983, p. 50) notes, 'to decipher the unknown language'. Too often counselling associated with Alzheimer's disease is either genetic counselling or is offered to the relatives or carers (who do of course have needs of their own) rather than to the patient. It seems that patients would at the very least benefit from counselling at the time of diagnosis and in the early stages of the disease to help them come to terms with the inevitable losses that they will face. It may well be the case that counselling could continue to be beneficial in the later stages where there is still a sense of self – this may be dependent to some extent on the medication used and its effect on cognition. More research needs to be done in this field, but once again we should not lose sight of the fact that we are dealing with people, with individuals who have different experiences and reactions.

Much of the aggressive behaviour exhibited by patients with Alzheimer's is related to the frustration of not being heard or being misunderstood – counselling may provide them with a space for this. Counselling, as we know, is concerned with feelings and emotions, which, it is now understood, have their memory situated in different areas of the brain to the episodic memory (the amygdala and hippocampus respectively). In line with memory rehabilitation, counselling can provide a safe and therapeutic environment for people with Alzheimer's disease to experience and express emotions and needs in a meaningful and supportive context of relationship that values the subjectivity of the individual (Kitwood, 1996). The most influential counselling technique we have is the way in which we develop, maintain and sustain a relationship. Therefore, counselling may be fruitful in many unexpected situations, providing a flexible and creative view of the concept of relationship is permitted. Oliver Sacks (1985) captures the essence of this message succinctly when he writes:

> In Korsakoff's, or dementia, or other such catastrophes, however great the organic damage and human dissolution, there remains the undiminished possibility of reintegration by art, by communication, by touching the human spirit: and this can be preserved in what seems at first a hopeless state of neurological devastation.

4.8   Many of the clients that I work with as a volunteer attend a day hospital and have learning disabilities. My supervisor is sceptical of the benefit of counselling to this client group. Should I continue to offer my support?

What is now called learning disability was previously classified as mental handicap or retardation and can either be quite mild, or so severe that living independently is not possible. This change of terminology is not just part of the move towards political correctness: it indicates a fundamental shift in understanding. Learning disability has often been confused with mental illness but is now recognised to be very different. Learning disability is a life-long condition that starts before adulthood and may be a result of genetic factors or damage to the brain, often at birth. The effect is usually permanent and sometimes physical development is affected too. Learning disability tends to be fairly fixed and cannot really be treated with medication. Mental health problems, on the other hand, are not usually evident in the early years of life (although some problems can appear in childhood), and the feelings and behaviours can either be temporary, or the person feels well for some of the time and unwell at other times. It is possible to completely recover from mental health problems and medication can, at times, be a useful tool.

Although learning disability and mental health problems are two separate diagnoses, people with learning disabilities, like anyone else, can experience the full range of mental health problems. In fact, according to the 'Mansell Report' (1993) people with learning disabilities are *more* vulnerable to mental health problems and psychiatric illness than the general population. This report estimates that up to 50 per cent of adults with learning disabilities also have mental health needs. This may be due to confusion over symptoms; for example, self-harming or 'challenging' behaviour can be the result of frustration and difficulty in finding a means of expression rather than other underlying psychological problems. However, medication is still the most frequently used approach to dealing with such problems (Matthews, 1995).

It is claimed that the use of DSM-IV and ICD-10 (see Question 2.7) has increased the reliability of the diagnostic process, but it is questionable whether symptom definition has the same validity for those with learning disabilities. One of the main problems is that people with learning disabilities are often not able to express their feelings easily in words. This difficulty in self-expression can result in poor diagnosis and depression may be under-diagnosed (Bouras, Holt & Gravestock, 1995) or challenging behaviour over-medicated (Bhaumik, Collacott, Gandhi & Duggirala, 1995).

People with a learning disability can experience mental health problems for the same reasons as the rest of the population; for example, depression can be triggered by a bereavement and a person with learning disabilities is likely to need sensitive support at times such as when a parent or close relative dies, or when a carer has to leave. Life changes too, such as changing school, at puberty, beginning work, starting to live independently, having a baby – all can produce increased anxiety. Counselling can be invaluable in offering support in the form of positive regard, as well as in helping prepare and support the client through these changes. Expressing feelings can be difficult for a client with learning difficulties, but is perhaps a necessary part of 'working through' a problem. A sensitive and imaginative counsellor can help with this, finding strategies such as pictures, storybooks, photos, drawings or drama as an alternative to the more conventional 'talking' therapy.

It is not just unconditional positive regard that is important. As with any client, all of what Rogers described as the 'core conditions' are especially necessary when working with clients who have learning disabilities. In this situation the counsellor needs to be sure that they can be congruent, or integrated in the relationship. Can they relate as person to person, with the flexibility that is necessary to communicate this when words are not the best medium? Can they experience a real empathy for the client's internal frame of reference? To do this we need to be in touch with our own disabilities, our own difficulties in communicating and understanding, and our own frustration about expressing ourselves fully.

When working with clients with learning disabilities contact may not be so easily verbalised but there can be a very powerful connection. The counsellor will have to rely on his or her own professional judgement or integrity to assess whether communication is, at least to a degree, being achieved. A counsellor working with clients who have a learning disability also needs to hone their observation skills; and after taking full account of the medical (developmental and physical) history, needs to be particularly vigilant for signs of change in the client's usual behaviour, for these are often the 'words' used to explain what is troubling them.

In general people with learning disabilities are more vulnerable to neglect and physical and sexual abuse because they cannot easily protect themselves, cannot tell others or are simply not believed. Abuse can lead to depression or other mental distress. Unfortunately counselling and psychotherapy are less common as a form of treatment than medication even though this group of people, theoretically, have the same rights as everyone else. Counselling and psychotherapy have an important role to play in the care of those suffering from depression and other mental distress, providing a space and opportunity to talk and be heard as well as attempting to find practical ways of improving the situation. It is clear that counselling and psychotherapy can then be very useful for clients with learning disabilities, *provided that approaches are adapted* to fit the individual's level of understanding and ability to communicate, and that the client's wishes are taken into account.

CHAPTER 5

Mental health and spiritual distress

5.1 What is the interface between mental illness and spiritual distress?

Professionals involved in therapeutic practices are familiar with the process of searching, evaluating and reconstructing important experiences undertaken by adults throughout their lives. Many therapists speak of modern man's widespread emptiness, isolation and unfulfilment (Gergen, 1991; Kohut, 1977). Nino (1997) argues that spiritual concerns are beginning to find an unusual resonance in contemporary society, evidenced by the plethora of books, journals and media coverage. He contends that the eagerness for the spiritual is also finding its expression through narratives of personal journeys and other reflective accounts. Counselling, he posits, is a time-honoured framework for listening to subjective spiritual quests through personal narratives. He suggests that most people have an innate idea of a personal 'ultimate other' or God, and that 'faith development and spirituality represent stages of a relation to this reality' (Nino, 1997, p. 195). Often, within counselling and psychotherapy, and indeed in everyday life, the spiritual dimension is treated as separate from other facets of the adult self, perhaps due to the sensitive and delicate nature of the material, which, it can be argued, both reaches and transcends the deepest aspects of the individual.

Throughout the ages people have turned to their religious or spiritual leaders for help and counsel. As the psychology of religion developed the relationship between mental illness and religion was studied, with Starbuck (1899) and Leuba (1896) asking such questions as 'Is conversion a sign of pathology or is it on the contrary an attempt to integrate an unstable self?' and 'To what degree are intense religious and mystical experiences connected with mental health or with psychopathology?' (Pieper, 2004, p. 349). Patients diagnosed with mental illness, as human beings, are also engaged in their own spiritual quest, and whilst spiritual matters and concerns are generally cultivated in privacy, or with close companions, those with mental illness, it seems, have a tendency to be less inhibited about many issues, including spirituality.

Explanations of mental illness need to include alternative perspectives from the traditional psychiatric ones, often derived from the DSM-IV (see Question 2.1) (Fee, 2000; Freshwater, 2003; Harper, 1995). Significantly, a religious or spiritual problem was a new diagnostic category in the 1994 *Diagnostic and Statistical Manual of Mental Disorders* (American Psychiatric Association, 1994). Defined as 'distressing experiences that involve loss or questioning of faith, problems associated with conversion to a new faith, or questioning of spiritual values that may not necessarily be related to an organised church or religious institution' (p. 843), it does not make explicit reference to meaning or purpose. Nevertheless, both clients and therapists should have the opportunity to enjoy a more flexible and creative choice in how to understand their experiences. One such perspective is that of spirituality, religion and faith. The National Institute for Mental Health in England (2004) has made a concerted effort to promote the importance of including the spiritual dimension in supporting those with a mental illness in the recently published *Promoting Mental Health: A resource for spiritual and pastoral care*. This was developed in collaboration with the Church of England and outlines, amongst other things, the protective effects that spirituality can have on mental health.

In our so-called 'secular' society it may be tempting to dismiss the relationship between mental illness and spiritual distress as increasingly irrelevant, but this is far from the case. Both the press and television recognise the current interest that there is around the interface between mental illness and spirituality. In April 2003, *The Times* newspaper featured an article written by Anjana Ahuja entitled '*God on the brain: is religion just a step away from mental illness?*' The focus of the piece was a television documentary (*Horizon*, God on the Brain, April 2003) that suggested 'religious feelings are brain malfunctions' and that 'some brains are physically built to be more receptive to divine thought' (Ahuja, 2003). The article continues 'God is an artefact of our evolved human minds, and visions are symptoms of neurological abnormality'. Further research by the neuroscientist Vilayanur Ramachandran has established a link between religious thought and the temporal lobes of the brain (Ramachandran & Hubbard, 2001, 2003). He claims, however, that his experiments do not devalue religious belief. Additionally, Canadian neurobiologist Michael Persinger (1999) also claims that his research shows that the brain creates religious experiences.

Religion is defined here as an organised set of beliefs that attempt to answer life questions through dogma, sacred texts, ritual and practices; but only the individual can come to know their own spiritual self as they search for meaning within their lives. For some people spirituality will not be entirely separate from religion, and it is important that as counsellors we do not make the mistake of thinking that all Moslems, or all Sikhs, or all Hindus view themselves in the same way in relation to their chosen religion. Historically, Freud (1926) characterised religion and spirituality as essentially products of illusion; that is, of wish-fulfilment. In *Civilisation and Its Discontents* (Freud, 1930) he reduces the 'oceanic experiences' of mystics to 'infantile helplessness' and 'regression to primary narcissism' and describes religion as 'a universal obsessional neurosis'. From a position that denies any legitimacy to religious or spiritual beliefs and experiences, one can only pathologise.

Jung (1964b), on the other hand, saw all psychological problems as essentially religious problems, and saw religious and spiritual beliefs and experiences as both meaningful and teleological. Furthermore, he suggested that healing is not possible without some sort of spiritual awareness, because the spiritual is equal in significance to the physical, emotional and cognitive. His influential text *Man and his Symbols* (1964a) was essentially a study of human beings and their spiritual problems. However, note that Jung's approach is open to the criticism that he elevated the beliefs and experiences of clients, even the most psychologically disturbed, to a spiritual status.

What is common to all spiritual or religious quests (and indeed psychological theories) is the notion that people have a deep desire to create meaning and purpose out of their lives and that disenchantment prevails when meaning is (temporarily) lost and meaninglessness ensues. It has been argued that our contemporary psychiatric and mental health disorders are due, in the main, to a loss of soul. Jung famously argued this point, as did Kopp (1991) and others. Moore (1996), for example, contends that we live in a disenchanted society, 'one that suffers the lack of a deep, solid, communal fantasy life'; whilst Yalom (1999, p. 5) opines that 'we are meaning seeking creatures... who must deal with the inconvenience of being hurled into a universe that intrinsically has no meaning'. The experience of a total lack of meaning is sometimes known as spiritual distress (see Question 5.4). Burnard (1987) defines spiritual distress as the total inability to invest life with meaning; he suggests that it can be demotivating, painful and cause angst for the sufferer.

Counselling and psychotherapy have often been described as meaning-making activities, latterly through the process of narrative and dialogue (Angus & McLeod, 2004). White (2004, p. 38) links the process of meaning making with psychotherapy and narrative, arguing that we are all 'impassioned meaning makers in search of plausible stories'. Nino (1997) identifies three major areas of psychological inner life that are essentially spiritual concerns and worthy of exploring. These are inwardness (or a return to self), relatedness and generativity. One might question the capacity of those with chronic and severe mental illness to have a consistent and constant awareness of their own inner life. This does not mean, however, that they are lacking in the spiritual concerns that are basic to all humankind, namely meaning and purpose.

Zinnbauer and Pargament (2000) suggest that there are four approaches within counselling to addressing religious and spiritual issues: rejectionist, constructivist, pluralist and exclusivist. Freud's view could be seen essentially as a rejectionist view, which reduced religion to the level of a psychological disturbance or a defence. Other examples of a rejectionist view include Albert Ellis's equating of religious belief with irrational thinking. In an interview (2001) Ellis, creator of Rational Emotive Therapy, stated 'Spirit and soul is horseshit of the worst sort. Obviously there are no fairies, no Santa Clauses, no spirits. What there is, is (sic) human goals and purposes...But a lot of transcendentalists are utter screwballs'. This aptly, and scarily, illustrates the clinical insensitivity of some therapists who use this approach to individuals who come with religious or spiritual problems or concerns of the soul.

A constructivist view denies the existence of an *absolute* reality but accepts that individuals construct their own meanings and realities. It is not essentially religious or atheistic. Such an approach allows counsellors to work with individuals from differing religious and spiritual backgrounds. The main concern with the constructivist view arises over where to draw the line between health and pathology, an important observation in regard to this chapter.

A pluralist approach recognises the existence of an absolute religious or spiritual reality but allows for different paths towards this, whereas an exclusivist, is respectful of a client's religious views if they conform to his or her own understanding of the 'one true' religion. An example of this may be found in some Christian counsellors who view more secular counselling approaches as contrary to their own value system and therefore misleading or dangerous (Adams, 1970 cited in Zinnbauer and Pargament, 2000; Bobgan & Bobgan, 1987).

As already mentioned people with a mental illness are often searching for meaning, questioning their identity, their place in the world, their purpose or potential, and also express spiritual needs, which may arise within a religious or non-religious frame. (A spiritual need is unique to that individual rather than common to one particular religion or another.) As discussed above, spiritual distress can be seen as an inability to find meaning in life with a resulting sense of loss and despair, and although it is not the same as clinical depression it may be a part of that state. It could also take the form of severe anxiety or feelings of alienation, extreme guilt or confusion about pain, suffering, life and death or indeed anger. All are indicators of spiritual distress and also of mental illness, and may interfere with the functioning of the individual leading them to seek help through counselling. To be aware of the spiritual aspect of a mental disturbance is not a secondary task but a fundamental part of the care offered, as indicated by mental health users in a study by Nathan (2001). Patients who participated in this study were of the opinion that 'when spiritual care is appropriately provided it can enhance the effectiveness of other aspects of care' (Rampes, 2004, p. 346).

It is unrealistic to expect that therapists should be well informed about the many different religions, as well as the diversity of mental illnesses, but if we can accept that each religion is an attempt to meet spiritual needs then permitting a 'spiritual' dimension will provide some freedom to work with clients from differing religious and spiritual backgrounds.

The spiritual, then, includes ideas such as purpose and meaning, love, caring, forgiveness, prayer, worship, belief (faith) amongst others, and is fundamental to the practice of both counselling and psychotherapy itself, even if the label is rarely used in that context. The challenge for practitioners is to hold in awareness the spiritual aspect of the presenting problem, which will invariably be obscured and most often unconscious.

While there does seem to be a relationship between mental illness and spiritual distress, for many people there is also a *positive* interface between mental health and spiritual well-being which tends to be ignored. Counselling is one space where such acknowledgements can and do take place, whilst also making a legitimate and thorough assessment of the client's mental state. As Zinnbauer and Pargament (2000, p. 162) urge: 'The clear need at present is for counselling approaches that do not pathologise or elevate client religious and spiritual beliefs without clear empirical or clinical justification. The fine line to be walked is between respect for client's beliefs and the need to treat legitimate psychopathology'.

5.2   My client, who has been referred to me by his GP, believes that he has been visited by the Holy Spirit and has been given powers of healing. He is a lay preacher and had a strong Christian faith but has resigned from his job as an executive director to attend to his calling. How can I be sure that he is not mentally ill?

It is not unusual for clients who have had a profound religious experience to be misdiagnosed with a mental health problem (Turner, 1995). However, patients with mental illnesses such as schizophrenia and other psychotic disorders of mood and perception often experience delusions that are religious in nature. Delusions are normally defined as false beliefs based on an incorrect interpretation of an external reality. It should also be noted that beliefs are culturally and socially bound (see question 4.1) and beliefs common to some groups can be misinterpreted as delusions. There are many different types of delusion, and diagnosis of mental illness relies, to some degree, on the differentiation of the type of delusion. In the situation outlined here, the counsellor might be concerned that the client is experiencing delusions of grandeur, or grandiose delusions. These involve the individual believing and feeling they have special powers, gifts or talents such as being able to heal the sick. Such beliefs are sometimes linked to religious delusions in which people interpret external behaviours as signs that God is trying to communicate with them. Occasionally people might believe themselves to be a renowned religious figure, saviour or prophet. Sufferers usually deny mental illness and often refuse psychiatric help, meaning that health professionals who are trained to be at the forefront of dealing with such issues are often the last to see them (Munro, 1999). Despite what might be viewed as outrageous behaviour, some delusional individuals manage to adopt a lifestyle that accommodates and sanctions their behaviour as in the case of the Reverend Bob Jones in the Jonestown Massacre.

The question of how to be sure that a client is not mentally ill is an interesting and challenging one. Joseph (2001) argues that there are no clear guidelines that help to distinguish between normal religious beliefs and pathological religious delusions. If we are to believe Freud (see Question 5.1) all religious beliefs are delusional [or as Jacobs (2000) argues, illusions]. Religious beliefs exist outside of the traditional scientific domain and can therefore easily be labelled as delusional when viewed from within a rationalist framework. There are, however, some guiding fictions to support the assessment and diagnosis of delusional beliefs. Greenberg and Witzum (1991) suggest psychotic experiences are:

- more intense than a religious experience
- often terrifying and pre-occupying for the individual
- associated with deterioration in client care of self
- often involve special messages from religious figures.

Joseph (2001) suggests that important considerations for clinical practice include the dimensional characteristics of the religious belief, such as its cultural influences and its impact on functioning. Lukoff (1985) adds that we should also take account of functioning prior to the episode, whether the onset of 'symptoms' is sudden and if there has been a stressful precipitant. Although the client in this question is ostensibly referring to the God (or Holy Spirit) of Christianity, each individual's experience of their God is personal and is affected by their personal history (see Question 5.1). As with all new referrals the counsellor should undertake a thorough and detailed assessment/history (see Question 2.7). In this case he or she will almost certainly want to explore the context within which the client has decided to follow his calling. A lack of attention to physical needs might verify the counsellor's concern that the client is mentally unstable. Past history of mental disorders would also be indicative, although not necessarily diagnostic, in determining the client's mental state. The image of the Holy Spirit is one of power and authority (the image is not quite patriarchal but carries with it the idea of obedience), and again it might be useful to hold this in awareness as the client describes his past and present experiences. Naturally, such information will be viewed in the context of whether or not the client has self-referred and the presenting problem. For example, the client may have chosen to engage in therapy as a way of validating his yearning to follow his heart's desire, which he may feel ambivalent about. It is also a very common human experience to question 'am I going mad?' in such circumstances. The client here is already a lay preacher and has a strong Christian faith. To become a lay preacher takes time, commitment and training and so this it seems is not a 'road to Damascus' experience coming completely out of the blue.

Jung (1987) might argue that the relativity of our own view of God is conditioned by our psychic development. One question that counsellors might ask themselves is: What else is going on in the client's life in terms of insecurity? In this case, as an executive director the client may be either middle-aged or feel he has reached the top in his career. Here the inquiry becomes a question of *why now?* What has happened to lead this particular image of God to emerge now?

The question of whether this belief is pathological or rather represents a true and deeper reality is therefore a sensitive and debatable one. And of course, we may never know. However, it is worth reflecting on the sociology of delusional beliefs and the way in which these are interpreted and managed within society. Palmer (2001, p. 120) reminds us that 'it is the most powerful person whose views are counted as real', and in psychiatry 'when a belief contrasts with objective reality it is the individual's problem and they who are irrational'. In other words, delusions are interpersonal phenomena which 'are rooted in an asymmetry of social power' (Palmer, 2001, p. 120). Counsellors and psychotherapists have positions of power and authority and as such have the opportunity to perpetuate dogma about what constitutes reality and how mental illness is constructed (see Chapter 4).

5.3   Why is it that psychotic clients tend towards spiritual themes during periods of mental breakdown?

Spiritual concerns are just one dimension of any mental (or indeed physical health) crisis and reflect the need for re-integration of projected aspects of the self and the desire for unconditional love and trust. Jung (1964) maintained that nearly all religious systems contain images that symbolise the process of individuation, whether this be Krishna, Buddha or Adam or Eve. Such archetypal images, it could be argued, are deeply embedded within our individual (personal) and collective psyche, both consciously and unconsciously. He also contended that psychological regulation is effected by religious and spiritual symbols and that the unconscious takes an interest in attempting to unite symbols of light and dark (such as God and the Devil), which have been polarised and possess the potential for transformation and individuation.

Existential therapists believe that life's most important questions are around the spiritual themes of identity, direction, meaning and purpose. Who am I? Why am I here? Where am I going? What does it all mean? Answers to these form a part of our own personal story or myth, the way that we live in the world. When these questions cannot be answered, sense cannot be made of the world, and functioning in that world can be severely impaired to the point of breakdown or failure to cope with the physical, emotional and intellectual demands of life. Transpersonal theories make for interesting reading in this area. Much of the literature originates from experiences of mainstream psychologists who, over a period of decades, have studied intense religious and altered states of consciousness, as for example in subjects who had ingested psychedelic drugs such as LSD or nitrous oxide (Grof, 1976; Masters & Houston, 1966). Many individuals relate profound spiritual experiences when under the influence of drugs, including experiences of being at one with the ultimate source of existence. Therapists have explained this as a result of the loosening of the primal repression of the spiritual, encouraged in the early stages of child development, and a 'reopening of experience to the non-egoic core' (Reading & Jacobs, 2002, p. 118).

It is not surprising then that individuals who are vulnerable to mental illness exhibit a more explicit connection to spiritual images and symbols. It could be argued that previously repressed and denied contents of the unconscious and the preconscious/conscious mind, which are normally kept under control by the moderating ego, are released as the ego loses its hold on the psyche. Other writers, however, such as Rowan (2002) or Wilber (2000) would argue somewhat differently, drawing a distinction between the pre-personal and the trans-personal, asserting that such experiences are rather about being in union with the larger whole, the ultimate, the universal spirit, etc.

It is interesting to note that some studies demonstrate a correlation between religious commitment and mental health (see, for example, Pieper, 2004). Tepper et al. (2001, p. 660) propose that 'religion may serve as a pervasive and potentially effective method of coping for persons with mental illness, thus warranting its integration into psychiatric and psychological practices'. Peiper (2004) in his latest study concurs with this sentiment and works to rehabilitate the negative pathologising of spiritual and religious themes manifest in psychotic patients so that they may be viewed as a more positive coping strategy. Gartner, Larson and Allen (1991) more specifically link what they call a 'lack of religiosity' to depression, noting that 'religiosity' protects against drug and alcohol misuse, which are commonly used as 'maladaptive' ways of dealing with depression.

Rejection and fear of people with mental illness have been commonplace across religions and cultures, and as already mentioned in Question 5.2, there are no easy distinctions between some forms of religious inspiration and symptoms of psychosis. Where people with mental illness do express a spiritual element to their disorder, it is not helpful for them to be discouraged from seeking professional help by religious groups, nor does it help for the mental illness to be explained as being caused by the individual's sins (National Institute for Mental Health in England, 2004). It is important to recognise the support that can be extended by faith communities to people with mental health problems. On the other hand, as is now commonly known, many individuals have been emotionally and psychologically damaged by their contact with and experiences of religious groups.

5.4   Some writers refer to the concept of a spiritual emergency when a client has a mental breakdown. What do they mean?

As previously noted, religious or spiritual problems are a new diagnostic category in the DSM-IV (see Question 5.1). Whilst there is extensive literature on the frequent occurrence of religious and spiritual issues in clinical practice, the impetus for the inclusion came from transpersonal clinicians whose initial focus was on spiritual emergencies. Spiritual emergency is variously defined, but in the main relates to forms of distress associated with spiritual practices and experiences (Lukoff, 1998). Watson (1994) describes three varieties of spiritual emergency, namely the visionary/mystical, the psychotic and the shamanic experience. Clearly the therapeutic interventions and approaches differ according to the presentation of the emergency. Patients in spiritual crises often appear to be chaotic and events seem to manifest as psychopathology, which Watson (1994) argues tends to denigrate and interrupt the process. Viewing a mental breakdown as a spiritual emergency creates the potential for mental traumas to be understood in a more valuable and depathologised manner, recognising the transformative potential inherent within the process; that is, the latent possibility of breakthrough is appreciated, rather than the focus being on the presentation of breakdown.

In a recent study of women's experience of spiritual emergency, many women experienced their crisis as transformative or life changing, despite the accompanying feelings of fear and pain and some pathological elements

(Lesniewicz, 2004). Unfortunately it is often the more extreme cases of spiritual emergency that reach the public domain and the negative effects of religion are pounced on by the press as particularly 'newsworthy'. Consider for example the incidence of mass suicides or schizophrenic auditory hallucinations that lead to violent and sometimes fatal outcomes. Distinguishing mystical and shamanic experiences from truly diagnosable and treatable psychosis is a highly sophisticated skill, and one based in experiential learning as opposed to learning through professional qualification alone. In the rush to diagnose and pathologise, it is tempting to make a simple equation of psychosis with spiritual excess, closing down the possible treatment options. Openness to new understanding, respect, and sensitivity are the key therapeutic skills when inviting discussion of spiritual and religious issues. The core conditions of counselling could perhaps be seen to embody if not a spiritual approach, one that is conducive to facilitating an exploration of spiritual matters.

CHAPTER 6

Working collaboratively to improve care[1]

6.1   There are a number of new roles being developed within the NHS mental health services. How do they link with counselling and psychotherapy as emerging professions?

It is estimated that at least 630 000 people in the United Kingdom are in contact with the mental health services at any one time, so it is not surprising that there has been an increased investment in developing those services. In the National Health Service (NHS) plan (Department of Health, 2000) the Government set out its vision for the modernisation of mental health care situated within primary care. Linked to the *National Service Framework for Mental Health* (NSF) (Department of Health, 1999a; see also Chapter 1), the plan identifies a number of new resources to support primary health care practitioners delivering high-quality, effective and timely mental health services. Since 2002, mental health services in the United Kingdom have been strengthened by the introduction of 50 early intervention teams, over 200 crisis resolution teams and the same number of assertive outreach teams. Further investment focuses on the development of new roles: the graduate mental health worker is one such resource, as is the gateway worker. Funding was made available for 1000 graduate mental health workers who were to be trained in brief therapy techniques *of proven effectiveness* (see Question 7.1). As such the new mental health worker is seen as a clinical practitioner who is able to support the general practitioner by providing brief problem-solving therapy, assessment and facilitation of referrals and self-help.

To date there has been considerable controversy over the new role, fuelled by a lack of clarity regarding training and responsibilities and how

---

[1] This chapter was written by Dawn Freshwater with contributions from Jeni Boyd.

the new practitioner will fit into existing teams that already have access to a practice-based counselling/psychology service. The guidance provided by the government is specific about the desired outcomes in regard to the new workers, but not prescriptive about roles and responsibilities. It recognises the local differences and variations and as such permits each local national health trust to develop the new roles in conjunction with their own existing services. This attention to local detail is of course commendable; however, it does raise issues in regard to the standardised training and development of the new practitioners.

According to Jenkins (2002) 'The actual training apparently involves a taught component of 1–2 days duration and placements on inpatient wards and Community Mental Health Teams'. This sounds like a crash course in mental health. The individuals once trained are expected to undertake a number of key tasks including:

- Performing and documenting a full psychosocial assessment including risk.
- Developing care plans with carers, patients and team members.
- Participating in implementing care plans.
- Ensuring that follow-up occurs and relevant information is seen by all concerned in the patient's care.

It is not surprising that concerns have been raised over the ethics, efficacy and safety of such a plan, not only by counsellors, but by other highly trained and well-qualified mental health workers. Bower, Jerrim and Gask (2004), in their report 'Primary care mental health workers: role expectations', highlight the disagreement and ambiguity around the new role in relation to the work undertaken by other mental health professionals such as psychologists and nurses. In response to this and other emerging issues in the development of the mental health workforce the Sainsbury Centre for Mental Health has produced a document entitled *The Capable Practitioner* (Lindley, O'Halloran & Juriansz, 2001). The emphasis in this document, which describes a framework of capabilities, is on the skills, knowledge, values and attributes required by the mental health workforce to deliver the mental health services envisioned within the NSF. The domains of the framework include knowledge, process of care, ethical practice and interventions. Whilst the capability framework provides a useful conceptual map to underpin skills development across mental health services, it has already been the subject of debate, criticism and redefinition (see, for example, Musselwhite, Freshwater, Schneider & Galvin 2004).

Another evolving role is that of the 'gateway workers'. Funding for 500 of these community mental health staff was made available in 2003/4. The specific role of the gateway worker is to improve access to specialised services, support 24 hour provision, liase with mental health and social services teams, A&E, NHS Direct and primary care and to involve service users and carers.

Whilst it is somewhat of a relief that the need for an increased workforce in mental health has at last been recognised, there is much doubt about whether this is the right answer. Other possibilities to consider would be to develop counselling skills training for nurses or invest more money in those mental health workers fully trained to deliver psychological therapies. However, it is important that the new workers are not seen as a threat; rather that they provide an opportunity to improve the quality of care offered. Indeed the new roles and the NSF for mental health hold the potential to improve communication and dissemination of information and thus improve access to effective treatments for patients. If used to develop information databases this could improve liaison between primary care, mental health teams, housing, education, police and other local services, including non-statutory or voluntary organisations and, of course, counsellors. This supports the premise that patients with mental health problems could benefit from more coordinated support at primary care level through a seamless and integrated service.

6.2   The *National Service Framework for Mental Health* (NSF) emphasises the role of counselling and counsellors in the management of acute and chronically ill patients. How will this affect counsellors in private practice?

The *National Service Framework for Mental Health* (Department of Health, 1999a) attempts to pull together a number of neglected areas in the care and management of the mental health of the population. It aims not only to serve those with acute and chronic mental illness, but also the general population, striving to integrate physical and psychological care and attend to the issue of health promotion and disease prevention. Focusing on the mental health needs of adults up to the age of 65, it is a significant policy document high-lighting the agenda for mental health services over the next decade. As with most major policy documents, the NSF received a mixed response on publication, not least due to its perceived neglect of evidence provided by service users. Nevertheless, it is fair to say that the NSF will exert a major influence in the shaping of mental health services for many years to come, impacting on all those involved with such services, including counsellors and psychotherapists (see also Chapter 1). The publication of the NSF was closely followed by a further significant government document that is unequivocal in its acceptance and acknowledgement of psychological therapies as a treatment option in mental illness, namely *Organising and Delivering Psychological Therapies* (Department of Health, 2004) (see also

Question 7.2). The implications of the now more widespread acceptance of counsellors and psychotherapists within the public health care system are of interest to the wider profession, but particularly to those working in private practice.

One could speculate that counselling services *per se* are likely to become part of, in the United Kingdom at least, a managed service commissioned by Primary Care Trusts (PCTs). As such counsellors in private practice may find themselves tendering for work, depending on the organisation structure of the counselling services within their locality. The determined drive towards privatisation of medical care through insurance companies, health care plans and so on will also impact the work of the private practitioner.

As explored in Chapter 3 there is a strong link between mental health and physical symptoms: frequent attendees in primary care settings often present with chronic somatisation of symptoms for which no physical aetiology can be established. It is well documented too that those suffering from long-term and debilitating illnesses, such as cardiac disease, multiple sclerosis, diabetes and cancer, are more prone to depression and anxiety. The acknowledgement of the increasing mental health problems nationally and globally, alongside the professionalisation of counselling and psychotherapy, has led to a substantial increase in the number of counsellors and psychotherapists located within primary and secondary care settings. In addition, existing health care staff are undertaking further training in counselling skills and also offer alternatives to more orthodox treatments. Counsellors within primary care and in acute hospital settings can assist in the management and care of individuals with chronic physical conditions, support their families and/or carers and also take referrals for individuals with a diagnosed mental illness.

6.3   What are the existing mechanisms for referral to acute psychiatric services?

As always there are local variations according to the actual structure of the mental health services within the area and across geographical boundaries. However, general guidelines outlined in the *WHO Guide to Mental Health in Primary Care* (WHO Collaborating Centre for Mental Health Research UK, 2000) suggest that referral to secondary mental health services should be considered:

• Where there is a risk of harm to self (suicidal intent) or harm to others.
• In the case of sudden deterioration of social, occupational and/or academic functioning, where the patient is unable to continue activities of daily living (for example, unable to leave the home or look after the children).

- Where there has been a recent onset of hallucinations, delusions (strange beliefs or fears), extreme agitation or bizarre behaviour, strange speech, extreme labile (unstable) emotional states.
- Where families or other agencies (schools, social workers, probation and housing services) have asked for help with strange, frightening and inexplicable behaviour changes such as withdrawal, suspiciousness, self-neglect.
- Where there is severe physical deterioration.
- Where specific psychotropic medication is indicated (such as lithium).
- Where primary care interventions and/or other options have been exhausted, or the therapeutic relationship with the patient has broken down.
- If the patient requests a referral.

There are further considerations in the case of children and adolescents:

- Where assessment is not suitable for primary care (for example, attention deficit disorder, psychotic symptoms).
- Where treatment is not suitable for primary care.
- If parent requests a referral.

Referral to other agencies may be necessary if there is/are:

- any form of suspected abuse
- school attendance problems
- suspected learning disability
- a suspected substance misuse problem.

Counsellors and psychotherapists of course also have their own guidelines, linked to ethical frameworks. Some of the basic principles outlined in the BACP Ethical Framework (British Association for Counselling and Psychotherapy, 2002) can be translated across to other health care settings. For example, BACP stresses that 'All routine referrals to colleagues and other services should be discussed with the client in advance and the client's consent obtained...' and that 'reasonable care should be taken to ensure that the referral will be likely to benefit the client' (British Association for Counselling and Psychotherapy, 2005a). In primary care or private practice, referral to acute psychiatric services normally comes from the GP rather than the practitioner. However, it is helpful for the counsellor to be aware of the local referral criteria so as to recognise situations where consultation with the doctor may be necessary, ensuring that the best possible help is being offered, and reducing the risk to which the patient (and counsellor) is exposed.

Other referral routes may be through accident and emergency departments at hospitals, through NHS Direct or through drop-in centres. Once again the situation is not uniform across the country and some hospitals, particularly district general hospitals, continue to have rudimentary liaison services often amounting to no more than an assessment service for patients following episodes of deliberate self-harm.

Any assessment of patients in crisis also involves gathering information about socio-economic factors or precipitating factors, such as changes or problems with housing, work or family, as these too may play a relevant part in the problem. Across the country primary care teams have developed different ways to integrate primary and secondary mental health care. Some services provide a link worker, usually a community psychiatric nurse, who has a key role in liaising between primary and specialist services. (Note: it is one of the suggested roles for gateway workers to work in partnership with specialised teams to develop referral protocols and identify action necessary to reduce risk, delays and waiting time. See Question 6.1.)

One final factor to be taken into account in the existing mechanisms for referral to acute psychiatric services is availability or waiting time. As stated, if the patient presents a risk to self or to others (or if there is a possible need for in-patient admission), then referral is made to the psychiatric services. However, psychiatric services often refer the patient to psychological treatment services (PTS) for adjunctive psychological treatment, which can mean waiting for several weeks for an initial assessment and several months for treatment.

6.4 I am currently working with a client who is also in regular contact with her community psychiatric nurse (CPN). How can I maintain good collaborative relations with the CPN, whilst also ensuring my client's confidentiality is not compromised?

Confidentiality is a fundamental requirement in all caring and health related professions. In counselling this involves the protection of personally identifiable and sensitive data from unauthorised disclosure. This is also true for CPNs and indeed GPs. Counsellors, like all health care practitioners, are expected to act in accordance with the trust placed in them by the client. Hence, disclosure of confidential client information is necessarily restricted to those occasions where either the client consents to such a disclosure or the client (or another) is deemed to be at risk if information is not shared appropriately.

Counselling services have become much more freely available and are often attached to other practitioners working within a locality such as a multidisciplinary team or voluntary agency. Individuals with mental health problems invariably need access to a wide variety of services if they are to make the most of their potential for recovery. Perkins and Repper (2004, p. 133) point out that recovery is about people's whole lives, not just symptom management. They argue that in order to facilitate recovery, rehabilitation services need to 'adopt a team approach' and 'ensure continuity across providers'. The answer to Question 2.3 emphasises that the aim of all professionals working within the field of mental health is to provide the best available care for each individual. Counselling is by nature quite isolationist, in that it is carried out in a contained space protected by contracted boundaries, one of which is confidentiality. In many cases confidentiality is the cornerstone of the work, allowing very difficult areas to be explored and reconciled in the safety of a therapeutic alliance. However, it is not the only way of working and in some cases working collaboratively with other professionals such as the general practitioner, the community psychiatric nurse, the social worker, the carer and occupational therapist ensures maximum support for the client (and also for the counsellor).

Cameron, Edmans, Greatley and Morris (2003) remind us that 'people and agencies who know relatively little of each other's worlds need to learn about different perspectives and find innovative ways of using that learning to achieve common goals, such as making real inroads into health inequalities'. To this end communication and clarification are perhaps the two watchwords. BACP's Ethical Guidelines (2005a) also acknowledge the need for quality interactions when working with colleagues, stating that 'the quality of the interaction between practitioners can enhance or undermine the claim that counselling and psychotherapy enable clients to increase their insight and expertise in personal relationships'.

By clearly identifying the different roles of each professional and by talking about how these interrelate, a more 'holistic' approach can be facilitated. This recognises the interplay of the different aspects of the individual's story, and consequently informs the support offered. This open and supportive communication can also help prevent any manipulation or 'splitting'.

The clients themselves should, of course, also be involved in the process, and a clear contract, with specific goals, can help to differentiate the responsibilities and concerns of the various professionals involved. Once again good supervision is crucial to this process (see the companion book on *Supervision* by Walker and Jacobs, 2004). With the current emphasis of the government on providing an integrated mental health service, working collaboratively is becoming increasingly important; and as different professionals work alongside each other so they will learn more about the nature and extent of other professional roles. Health professionals are notoriously territorial in regard to their case management and workload, whilst simultaneously lamenting their lack of time and support. Suspicion and perceived threat often arise out of ignorance, so counsellors have a responsibility to ensure that others know what part counselling can play in the care plans for those who have mental health problems; they also need to learn about other professions. In short, difference is something to be engaged in rather than moved away from, and in doing so much common ground can be discovered and shared.

Naturally, the sharing of ideas and best practice is also the domain of health care managers as well as practitioners, and requires good role modelling and support through funding to ensure that liaison and collaboration are given the space and time they deserve, and that they do not take the form of snatched conversations in the corridor.

6.5   As a voluntary counsellor in a health centre how should I prioritise the counselling waiting list given that many of the clients are also awaiting a hospital appointment for an acute outpatient assessment?

Many counsellors and trainee counsellors provide voluntary services across a variety of NHS settings, by far the majority being attached to health centres and Primary Care Trusts. It is important for all parties that the counsellor is not just seen as an add-on but should have received a good induction into the processes and protocols of the practice. An introduction to the other staff with a clarification of roles, provided by the practice manager or line manager, might also be useful. This can include conversations about professional issues such as: what constitutes a suitable referral, agreement about the limits of confidentiality and collaboration with the referring GP or other referring professional if applicable (see Henderson, 1996). Counsellors should also expect to be included in, and be willing to attend, all practice meetings as part of the primary health care team. Once this is established then decisions such as this one concerning prioritisation on waiting lists no longer become the sole concern and responsibility of the counsellor. This is probably the most important piece of learning for counsellors, who can at times forget that they are working alongside colleagues and experts, who can provide advice and guidance on such matters. For example, the counsellor might discuss individual cases and the sense of urgency with the referring GP or community psychiatric nurse. Often, once the counsellor has contacted the client on the waiting list, the client is either in less of a crisis and decides not to take up the offer of counselling, or has begun other treatment, in which case the decision has already been made. With improved communication and a sense of being part of a team, this information may enable the voluntary counsellor to make the best use of the precious time allocated for counselling.

6.6 The social work team have made a referral to me as a trainee counsellor/social worker. The client is known to be a persistent non-attendee and has behavioural difficulties. Am I obliged to take the referral?

For basic principles of referral, the trainee social worker/counsellor is referred to the local policies and procedures. However, in the main, no professional is obliged to take a referral about whom they feel uncomfortable. Naturally, the reservations and reticence experienced by the trainee should be discussed and examined in detail in supervision and perhaps in caseload management meetings. Trainees, and to a certain extent qualified counsellors and social workers, do not say no often enough: it is one of the personal boundaries that is most difficult to promote. There is a temptation to be seduced into the role of rescuer; 'I will succeed where others have failed'. Where the trainee does decide to undertake counselling with a difficult client, extra support and supervision should be in place. What is also important with such clients is that the purpose of counselling is clearly outlined and understood and that it is offered alongside services that offer advice and support for practical living problems. Unless all these elements are in place there will be unrealistic and unrealised expectations about what counselling can achieve.

It is essential that clear boundaries are maintained in cases such as this, with a written contract regarding attendance and behaviour agreed from the first session. As counsellors and social workers, we live in the 'real' world and despite our best intent, it is not uncommon to come across the 'unpopular patient'. Social workers, GPs, nurses and counsellors alike have what they call 'heart sink' or 'thick note' patients, and those who are overworked and stressed may well attempt to pass these on. Once again with clear communication and clarification of roles, and a full and proper induction into the community team, clear referral protocols can be established for any member of staff. These can then, at least, be used as an explanation for the refusal to take the referral, if inappropriate.

6.7 Having completed the specified number of sessions with my client in an NHS setting, I feel that he requires further counselling. Should I offer him additional private sessions?

According to the BACP Ethical Guidelines (2005a) one of the fundamental values of counselling and psychotherapy is 'striving for the fair and adequate provision of counselling and psychotherapy services'. This question raises a number of tangential but related issues concerning the ethical principles of autonomy and beneficence and non-maleficence. It cuts right to the heart of counselling, in that it refers directly to the integrity of the counsellor–patient relationship, whilst adding the complexities of both setting and politics. One of the most difficult issues for counsellors working within the NHS is that of time constraints, driven by financial considerations, including the lack of funding for both short- and long-term services.

Evidence for best practice is far from conclusive regarding many forms of counselling and psychotherapy particularly concerning services in primary care (see also Question 7.1). In many cases the arbitrary limit set on number of sessions is based on cost rather than need (Parry, 1997). As Burton (1998, p. 210) notes 'There is little clinical sense in purchasers imposing arbitrary funding limits, or funding only a preset number of sessions, since the right dosage of psychotherapy varies according to the severity and complexity of the condition'. Whilst prescribing a pre-set number of sessions might on the surface appear cost-effective, it could be argued that individual differences and needs are disregarded, that little credence is ascribed to the value of the therapeutic relationship and further that the difference between efficacy and effectiveness is not recognised.

Aside from the ethical and practical considerations, there are also theoretical considerations. Neither the person-centred nor psychodynamic approach aligns itself easily with the current NHS ethos of a quick cost-effective fix. Some theorists, however, believe that the short time frame afforded to time limited counselling is not necessarily antitheoretical or inefficient. Yalom (1999, p. 113), for example, wonders if his client entered deeply into therapy '*because* of, not despite our limited time frame' (italics in the original). He points out that there is a long tradition in psychotherapy going back to Carl Rogers and, before him, to Otto Rank, which understood that a pre-set termination date often increases the efficiency of therapy. Jacobs (1999, pp. 156–157) adds that faced with the practicalities of working within a limited time frame the counsellor can 'make a virtue out of necessity . . . by using the ending constructively'.

Once a counsellor enters into a therapeutic alliance with a client, there are a number of basic ethical principles that hold true, that is to say that there are constants that transcend the issue of setting and context. These, simply stated, are *trustworthiness* (or fidelity), *autonomy* (which relates directly to the client's commitment/consent to be in counselling), *beneficence* (that the counsellor is acting in the best interests of the client) and *non-maleficence* (that the counsellor is not exploiting the client).

One of the ethical implications of this question perhaps concerns the possibility of a counsellor in independent practice 'persuading' a client that they need further counselling in order to earn more money. Or perhaps, that the client is in need of further work and might not feel able to refuse his current counsellor's offer in preference for a new referral. The counsellor/ client might also be concerned about the changing boundaries and expectations moving from one service to another.

Counselling within the NHS is usually offered on a time-limited basis, and of course this should be made clear in the initial contract. BACP's Ethical Guidelines (2005a) echoes this sentiment arguing that 'clients should be adequately informed about the nature of the services being offered'. However, it is not often apparent at the beginning of a counselling relationship whether or not 6–8 sessions will be sufficient. Once this *is* recognised the counsellor should find an early opportunity to discuss the implications and alternative possibilities within the current provision offered. At times engaging in counselling through private practice appears to be the best option, and indeed often it is the only option available.

Many clients *do* express a wish to continue counselling beyond the short-term work provided by the NHS and naturally a substantial proportion do not wish to start all over again with another counsellor. Yet, they are also not necessarily aware of the other options and what other counsellors might offer that is different. This should at least be addressed in the decision-making processes and can be done in a number of ways, for example by providing them with an independent list of counsellors within the area and a copy of the BACP information sheet about choosing a counsellor. The principle behind this is one of 'informed choice'. From the counsellor's point of view, supervision once again plays an essential role with its opportunity to explore any 'hidden' agendas.

If the client chooses to remain with their present counsellor, and the counsellor agrees to this, then a new contract is necessary. This contract refers to 'professional' as much as 'ethical' issues. Working in a time-limited way tends to be more focused or goal-oriented. It has a clear end that is signalled from the start. Longer term counselling tends to be more open-ended, allowing issues to evolve until there is a mutual agreement to end. This should be reflected in the new counselling contract.

Perhaps more attention needs to be given to selecting (or assessing) which patients would benefit from short-term and those who need long-term therapy, instead of a one size fits all policy? Parry (1999, p. 18) concludes that 'counsellors should not be debating for either brief or open-ended style in primary care, but should be organising themselves into extending the service to give GPs the choice of both approaches'.

There are also other professional issues to be addressed and again supervision is invaluable in offering a space to explore these as they may be hidden or masked. There can be sadness and frustration that the time limits set have let down both the client and the counsellor; and anger too that the system prevents the continuation of work. Finally, when working within NHS settings, counsellors are part of a team and concerns about ending can be shared, referral pathways explored and responsibility apportioned. Some GPs will re-refer so that therapy becomes intermittent – still time limited but extended by these re-referrals. In the 'real' world of waiting lists and of time and cost restraints perhaps one way forward is more open dialogue with the patients concerning the number of sessions and how this is affecting working together.

CHAPTER 7

Professional and legal matters[1]

7.1 As a psychodynamic counsellor working in primary care I am being asked to undertake training in short-term cognitive–behavioural therapy (CBT). Is there any evidence to suggest that either short-term CBT or psychodynamic work is effective with clients who have depressive/anxiety disorders?

Cognitive–behavioural therapy (CBT) aims to help the individual change patterns of thinking or behaviour that are causing them problems. Sessions are usually weekly and last for an hour, with the average number of sessions being approximately 10. CBT is now widely available and is provided by a broad range of health professionals as well as by qualified and experienced counsellors and psychotherapists. In broad terms psychodynamic therapies aim to help the individual understand more about themselves and their relationships. It is usually long term but is increasingly becoming an option for short-term work. It is interesting to note that despite psychodynamic therapy being more established than CBT, more research has been conducted on CBT than on any other therapy. Hence, although there is evidence to suggest that CBT is helpful in treating a variety of mental health problems including depression and anxiety, this does not necessarily prove that CBT is any better than the other therapies available. Rather, it is an indication that other therapeutic approaches have not been subject to the depth and breadth of research that CBT has.

The issue of evidence based practice in counselling and psychotherapy is currently a topic of contentious and polarising debate. There are many reasons for this. The National Institute for Clinical Excellence (NICE) uses

---

[1] This chapter was written by Dawn Freshwater with contributions from Jeni Boyd.

evidence of worth as the criterion for funding research and development: put simply if a service cannot provide evidence of worth then no (or very little) money will be spent on providing or improving those services. The 'gold standard' for gathering evidence of worth is the randomised controlled trial (RCT), which seems to work well for establishing the utilitarian value of what may be called 'cure' conditions such as diabetes, heart disease or cancer. Thus, in some cases the RCT is the obvious choice for determining evidence, particularly where consistent measurable treatments such as titrated medication and measurable effects such as blood pressure or blood sugar can be monitored. Mental health services, however, are less easily quantified, given that they are more concerned with 'care', which is not so easily measured by trials.

These are not the only problems: it might, at first glance, seem simple to state whether a psychological treatment has been delivered, but this is actually not so easy. What constitutes a 'dose' of counselling? Does a one-hour session of counselling constitute adequate treatment? These are not new questions; however, the dispute around efficacy in psychological therapies has been brought into sharp focus since the mid-1990s with the drive towards research based practice. In 1986 Howard, Moras, Brill, Martinovich and Lutz found a linear relationship between the number of sessions of any counselling and the probability of improvement: by the eighth session almost half of the patients had improved, and by session 26 half of the remaining patients had improved again. This 'dose-effect' finding has been replicated in other studies: Kopta, Howard, Lowry and Beutler (1994), for example, noted that 75 per cent of chronically distressed patients improved by session 52. Burton (1998, p. 210) sensibly questions the clinical sense in imposing arbitrary limits on funding or number of sessions since 'the right dosage of psychotherapy varies according to the severity and complexity of the condition'. As a corollary, it would be interesting to ask how patients would react if they were told that they were only entitled to a six weeks' prescription of antidepressants?

The NHS, however, does at least recognise some of these limitations and in their review of evidence pertaining to treatment length, they state that therapies of fewer than eight sessions are 'unlikely to be optimally effective for most moderate to severe mental health problems' (www.nelmh.org, accessed May 2005). Instead 16 sessions or more are recommended for relief of symptoms and there is recognition that 'longer therapies may be required to achieve lasting change in social and personality functioning'. It is acknowledged that some service commissioners have only been prepared to fund very brief therapies (six sessions) despite the lack of research evidence to suggest that this is an adequate trial of therapy. This applies both to short-term cognitive–behavioural therapy and to short-term psychodynamic work.

A further problem is encountered regarding evaluating the efficacy of counselling once one begins to question how change can be measured. Emotional distress such as depression and/or anxiety cannot easily be calculated, except through self-reporting, which in turn provides a challenge to the validity of RCTs. This alone poses a challenge to the existing measures of mental health used to classify and label disorders in the first instance. These are claimed to be both 'reliable' and 'valid' but can only ever be based on the subjective experience or self-reporting. Perhaps the biggest question mark hangs over the issue of causality of change. Stone (1993) reported that change depends less on type or length of therapy, rather on varying character traits such as 'motivation, the strength to face weakness, the confidence to trust another person and the flexibility to weigh and select'. Saunders (2000) also found that an emotional connection that is empathic and positive and a mutual understanding with the therapist are as important in recovery as a specific intervention.

Curtis Jenkins (2002) writes of the special problems relating to counselling research. Apart from the problems with randomisation (seen in RCTs) and the easy and varied manipulation of selection, he also cites sample size as critically important, as small numbers in randomised or control groups can distort or overestimate effects. He observes: 'This is an ever present hazard to research into counselling in primary care which normally fails to attract funding of sufficient size to ensure that the numbers of patients in the sample "arms" are large enough to prevent this happening' (2002, p. 201). In addition, he contrasts counselling with a drug, stating that it cannot be applied in 'appropriate measured doses to a consistently behaving patient with a specific problem'. Each case is individual and counsellors and psychotherapists know that they have to tailor the 'treatment' to each patient to meet their specific needs.

Cummings and Sayama (1995) state that counsellors report using a combination of different therapeutic approaches. To quote Curtis Jenkins (2002, p. 201) again: 'The reality is that most psychotherapy researchers now reluctantly agree that therapists themselves are more likely to be the cause of outcome variance than the style of therapy offered'. This has obvious implications for small-scale RCTs where two or three therapists could contribute to half the total treatment effect. Jenkins cites Ward et al. (2000) claiming their conclusions are erroneous: in his words 'very unsafe'.

Indeed the Department of Health guidelines (2004) indicate that the effectiveness of all types of therapy depends on the patient and therapist forming a good working relationship. RCTs, by definition, exclude patient choice yet are still regarded as 'the way' to research psychological therapies. These inherent contradictions are not arbitrary; rather they have significant implications for the findings and recommendations of the current research in counselling and psychotherapy efficacy. Moreover, it is important to realise that findings based on such contradictory foundations are the basis for implementing policy guidance about, for example, short-term therapies.

Saunders considers the findings of both individual research evidence and various meta-analyses (whereby a number of individual research studies are summarised, integrated and compared). The conclusion he seems to arrive at is that 'short term dynamic therapy is as effective as other treatment' and that 'psychotherapy had a "mean effect" size that was considerably larger than that of a plethora of widely used well established medical interventions, such as heart by-pass surgery' (2002, p. 246).

In terms of evidence supporting short-term psychodynamic work, Burton writes of the 'proliferation' of shorter term or brief psychodynamic therapies stating that 'a recent meta-analysis of 26 studies has shown them to be comparable in effectiveness to other treatments including cognitive behavioural therapy, and most effective when therapists are specifically trained in short-term models' (1998, p. 65). However, she queries the 'uncritical headlong rush into un-researched brief and ultra-brief psychotherapies' (1998, p. 65). Thereby questioning not only the false cost savings but also the ethics of such an approach where 'in the long term ... the emotional costs are borne by the patients' (1998, p. 209).

In 'Empirically-Validated Treatments *not* Empirically Valid' (www.talking-cure.com), the authors (Lambert and Bergin) criticise the early claims that CBT is more effective than other approaches in the treatment of anxiety based problems. They argue that they have 'upon later and more sophisticated analysis, largely proven to be the result of the highly reactive nature of outcome measures employed in such studies and the allegiance of the experimenters to the methods being employed' (Lambert & Bergin, 1994).

Given this discussion, some of the specific research that is available does raise a number of interesting points. Simpson, Corney, Fitzgerald and Beecham (2000) conducted a randomised controlled trial to evaluate effectiveness and cost-effectiveness of counselling for patients with chronic depression and found that there were similar improvements for both CBT and psychodynamic counselling. However, they recognised both the small population sample and the fact that the therapy in the study tended to be short term 'typical of most general practice counselling, but that longer term and more intensive therapy might possibly result in added benefits above GP care for the more severely depressed'.

In a trial of non-directive counselling, cognitive–behaviour therapy and usual general practitioner care in the management of depression and anxiety as well as mixed anxiety and depression in primary care, King et al. (2000) concluded that: 'In primary care settings, non-directive counselling and cognitive behaviour therapy were both significantly more effective than usual GP care in the short term. However there were no differences between these three treatments in either clinical outcomes or cost at the twelve month follow-up'.

Churchill et al. (2001) similarly supported the use of psychotherapy interventions stating: 'Patients receiving any variant of psychotherapy were significantly more likely to improve...and experienced greater symptom reduction...than those receiving treatment as usual'. The trials which compared different methods 'yielded insufficient data upon which to base firm conclusions'. In spite of this statement they conclude 'it would appear that some forms of brief psychological treatments, particularly those derived from cognitive/behavioural models, are beneficial in the treatment of people with depression being managed outside hospital settings'.

The National Electronic Library of Mental Health (www.nelmh.org) also quotes some earlier studies (Anderson & Lambert, 1995; Crits-Christoph, 1992; Svartberg & Stiles, 1991, 1993) reporting that two of these three high-quality reviews of the efficacy of short-term psychodynamic psychotherapy found it to be of similar effectiveness to other modalities. These reviews included mixed patient groups, including many patients considered difficult to treat, and concluded that these differences in findings may relate to different inclusion criteria.

Saunders (2002, p. 247) recognises the reality of the actual practice of counselling and psychotherapy and highlights the difference between efficacy judgements based on a controlled research environment and effectiveness in everyday life, stating that 'efficacious treatments are not equally effective with all people or all conditions'. What is clear, however, is that whatever scientific methods are used to investigate counselling and psychotherapy, it is consistently shown that psychological therapies offer something that 'works'. Compared with no treatment or with other treatment (including medication) it is shown to be effective. *Effectiveness Matters* (Glanville & Lefebvre, 2001), the update provided by NICE, reports that, in the short term (up to six months), 'counselling can be useful in the treatment of mild to moderate mental health problems' (such as anxiety and depression) and in the longer term (8–12 months) 'there are no differences in outcome between counselling and usual GP care' (which includes support from the GP in normal consultations, medication and referral to mental health care services). In other words counselling is *equally as effective* as these other treatments. Research, however, it seems, is not enough and there is a great need to disseminate information and educate those who commission and provide services for mental health in primary care about the value of counselling and psychotherapy for (amongst others) clients who have depressive/anxiety disorders.

It is important in any research, or review of research, including that in this chapter, that any bias is acknowledged in order to estimate the rigour and trustworthiness of the account. Counsellors and therapists are therefore encouraged to be reflexive; to become researchers into their own practice and to determine empirically the effectiveness of the interventions offered.

This of course is common practice through what Casement (1985) has called the 'internal supervisor', and therapists should not be put off by this call; they are 'natural researchers'. The criticisms cited here are not attempts to undermine research but rather, on the contrary, to make it *more* important and relevant to all who work in counselling or psychotherapy, and to highlight the importance of the gap between theory and practice.

7.2 What is the current model of choice for working with clients who have a history of mental illness?

In *Organising and Delivering Psychological Therapies* (Department of Health, 2004), the executive summary begins with the unequivocal statement that 'psychological therapies are part of essential healthcare. There is overwhelming evidence for their effectiveness in treating a wide variety of mental health problems and illnesses'. It is also acknowledged that no single therapy or type of practitioner can provide effective treatment for all the mental health difficulties experienced (see also Chapter 6 and Question 7.1). In February 2001 the government published their guidelines 'Treatment Choice in Psychological Therapies and Counselling'. However, whilst acknowledging that psychological therapies may be helpful, a number of conditions are excluded from the recommendations. These include those with a history of mental illness such as schizophrenia, mania and bipolar disorder, those with alcohol or other drug addictions and those with learning difficulties, even though these are often associated with mental ill health. In fact the whole issue of dual diagnosis seems to be marginalised.

As will be clear from other responses to questions (see question 7.1 specifically), it is difficult to base any psychological treatment choice on substantial evidence. Nevertheless, in *Improving Quality in Primary Care: A Practical Guide to the NSF for Mental Health* (Department of Health, 1999c), it is claimed that CBT is the 'treatment of choice for many common disorders such as depression, anxiety disorder, eating disorders and some somatic complaints'. Also included is an interesting observation that, although there is much evidence for the effectiveness of CBT in secondary care, 'the evidence is less strong in primary care'. The report continues by acknowledging that counselling 'may be as effective as CBT for some anxiety and depression problems, although it may not be of great benefit for more chronic depressive problems'. No distinction appears to be made between a single incident and those with a history of these conditions, nor are the claims justified by traditional scientific evidence.

As pointed out in Question 2.10, therapists approach the suitability of therapy with severe or long-term mental illness from a variety of viewpoints: the work of Jung and Laing, amongst others, promoted the value of talking therapies with even the most severely distressed and disturbed individuals.

Although clinical guidelines produced by the National Institute for Clinical Excellence (NICE) do not recommend counselling and psychotherapy as interventions in the routine care of people with schizophrenia, other psychological interventions of proven efficacy are indicated and available. There is now more evidence that people diagnosed as schizophrenic, and labelled 'medication resistant', when treated with CBT or supportive counselling, are found to have superior outcomes than those receiving routine care. Naturally service user preferences should be taken into account, especially if other more efficacious psychological treatments are not locally available.

The NHS National Electronic Library for Mental Health (www.nelmh. org) also notes that depressive disorders may be treated effectively with psychological therapy, with best evidence for cognitive–behavioural therapy and interpersonal therapy, and some evidence for a number of other structured therapies, including short-term psychodynamic therapy. This recommendation reflects a large body of research, considered in eight high-quality reviews and two Cochrane reviews: the best evidence is claimed for cognitive–behavioural therapy and interpersonal therapy. However, as described in the answer to Question 7.1, comparisons show few significant differences between orientations, and it is acknowledged that 'a number of other approaches have shown some evidence of effectiveness'. These include behavioural therapy, problem-solving therapy, group therapy, systemic therapy, non-directive counselling in primary care and psychodynamic interpersonal therapy.

The British government does acknowledge that for many patients with long-term mental illness, primary care is their sole point of contact with the NHS. But the care offered to these people is often poor due to limited resources, and too often there is a difference between appropriate care and availability. The assumption that a little help is better than no help can lead to the over-use of counselling or other short-term treatments.

Thus, it is important to remember that not all patients are suitable for brief or time-limited therapy, particularly those with a history of early development that is marked by deaths, separations, trauma or abuse (physical, sexual or emotional). One reason for this is that a particular function of therapy for these individuals is fostering the development of trust and allowing a secure attachment to another person to form. It is inappropriate, and possibly damaging, for such people to become dependent on those who cannot meet their needs, such as a counsellor who is only able to offer six sessions.

This situation often occurs when the patient's difficulties do not match the problem for which they were referred (that is, the presenting problem is not the real issue). On the surface there may appear to be a relatively simple problem, but as we know this often masks more complex factors that emerge later. Burton (1998, p. 209) contends that 'applying an Elastoplast to the most superficial problem and discharging the patient is no longer sufficient, although regrettably this continues to happen'. Such patients often become 'frequent attendees' in primary care, presenting with various symptoms, with the consequence that they become a 'revolving door case' resulting in intermittent therapy of short bursts. One answer is to offer further counselling privately (see Question 6.7). However, those with a history of mental illness may not always have the financial resources to choose this option. Further, it is questionable, ethically, to expect patients to pay for a treatment that the NHS itself states is an essential part of mental health care.

In a similar vein, not all patients will benefit from long-term psychotherapy and will be better off managed by community mental health teams and social support; but too often patients are fitted in to what is available, rather than being provided with the most effective therapy for their difficulties. Unfortunately provision, like research, is dominated by questions of short-term cost-effectiveness, and as stated elsewhere the real cost is borne by the patients who do not receive the essential care that is promised.

7.3   I am a counsellor in General Practice and have been sent (or received) some information on a training course in psychosocial interventions. How will this enhance my current counselling practice?

Mental ill health is frequently linked to a variety of factors. For example, the NHS report 'Fast Forwarding Primary Care Mental Health' (http://www.dh.gov.uk/assetRoot/04/06/11/12/04061112.pdf) makes links between people with severe mental illness and poor physical health: a poor diet, high risk of unemployment, increased risk of social exclusion, significantly lower incomes, and a greater likelihood of substance misuse and of smoking than the general population. In spite of the evidence for the effectiveness of psychological therapies and/or appropriate medication, these patients frequently re-present with different problems at primary care level. Typically, such patients account for high levels of service use. Expenditure is also higher for these patients than for other groups because of the cost of medical investigations.

The relationship between mental health and physical illness is discussed in depth in Chapter 3. This group may experience similar difficulties, especially those with chronic or recurrent conditions. Chapter 4 highlights the specific problems of ethnic and other minority groups, the elderly and those with learning disabilities – all of whom have a higher incidence of severe mental illness and the consequent problems posed by coping in society. The NHS recognises the levels of unmet need in these groups and its mental health taskforce is developing a strategy to tackle these issues. Quite clearly primary health care intervention, whether it is pharmaceutical or psychological treatment, is not enough and, as detailed in Chapter 6, collaborative working is encouraged between health and social care. The Health Act (1999) enables health and local authorities to pool their budgets in order to facilitate an effective partnership between health and social care by commissioning and providing psychosocial interventions.

The term 'psychosocial' acknowledges the complex interrelationship between the psychology of the individual and the social or interpersonal context. Psychosocial interventions are concerned with the psychological (including the emotional and spiritual) well-being of the patient *and* their family and/or carers, including issues of understanding and insight into their specific condition and social functioning, namely communication and adaptation to life within the family and the community (participation and integration), and relationships. One part of this care includes psychological therapies, which allow the patient and those close to them to express their thoughts and concerns, their feelings and fears relating to the mental illness that confronts them. Counsellors, however, should be aware that this is not always enough, and practical support and information is also needed. Mental health care cannot be viewed in isolation, and some knowledge of the other areas of help available allow the counsellors to concentrate on the psychological interventions and not be distracted by social concerns that are better dealt with elsewhere. It is by working collaboratively that individual needs can be identified, goals set and plans made to implement the care required. It is important to include the users and the carers in this collaboration; they know the problems and this simple act of inclusion in the process can be extremely important and empowering.

Psychosocial intervention courses generally include information about psychological and social interventions that will help people with severe mental illness and their (informal) carers to cope more effectively. The Clinical Resource and Audit Group (CRAG) outlines the following aims for psychosocial interventions for people affected by schizophrenia:

- assessment
- support
- explanation and education
- building concentration
- reinforcement of reality
- help with relationships and communication

- treatment of non-psychotic symptoms such as anxiety
- dealing with challenging behaviour, e.g. self-harm, aggression
- structuring the day
- attending to daily living skills
- working with families.

Where there is persistent and severe mental illness, an Assertive Outreach Team may be commissioned to assess the situation (including risk to the patient and others) and to arrange for evidence-based interventions, such as counselling, to promote recovery. They also offer practical and emotional support and arrange physical health checks with GPs, dentists, opticians, nutritionists or other specialists. They liaise with other agencies in the local environment to build support networks, and to encourage participation and integration into the community. The team consists of health and social services staff and is an example of the move towards working collaboratively.

In terms of enhancing current practice, all continuous professional training opportunities should be evaluated in relation to current expertise and practice, to identified gaps and needs in skills and of course to personal interest and future development. Psychosocial intervention training adds value to a counsellor's repertoire of skills and expertise, expanding awareness of the broader work required for individuals to make a lasting change in often deeply entrenched problematic social and familial contexts.

7.4 As a counsellor working in private practice are there any training courses that would help me to work better with mental illness?

The wealth of training courses that are now available for counsellors and psychotherapists can make it quite difficult to ascertain the most appropriate and relevant route to take. In the main, training and education that is available for counsellors and psychotherapists cuts across private practice, NHS and other public sector work, focusing instead on generic skills training, theoretical understanding and the establishment of ethical and professional standards. Such training relies on individual practitioners with support from their colleagues to transfer their learning into their own unique context.

There are also many specialised training courses available, which focus on specific illnesses and their management/treatment. The Counselling and Psychotherapy Forum for Primary Healthcare, established in 1999 by a number of interested parties including BACP, the Counselling in Primary Care Trust, Counsellors and Psychotherapists in Primary Care and UKCP, was set up to look at the diverse nature of training for primary care counsellors.

It was tasked with setting standards for education, training and professional development of counsellors, psychotherapists and psychologists working in primary care. Whilst recognising that the therapeutic alliance is 'a critical factor in counselling', the Forum suggests that generic training courses should include:

- assessment (risk and mental health)
- ethical and legal issues
- management of practice
- knowledge of mental illness
- sexual issues.

Most generic counsellor training includes ethical issues, and one of the main ethical considerations to always be borne in mind is competence. The ethical principle of beneficence 'directs attention to working strictly within one's limits of competence and providing services on the basis of adequate training or experience' (British Association for Counselling and Psychotherapy, 2002, p. 3). Regular supervision helps the monitoring and review of practice and provides a space to consider continuing professional development (CPD) in the light of new knowledge needed, changing circumstances and the specific client group, encouraging counsellors and therapists to engage in appropriate educational activities.

Working with those who have mental health problems whether in private practice or in the public sector usually brings a counsellor into contact with other mental health care services. It is useful to identify basic areas of knowledge and training for each specific setting. In many cases primary care settings act as a 'bench-mark' against which to measure competence, given that this is where the most acute and enduring mental health patients present.

The minimum requirements for primary care specific training are knowledge of:

- psychotropic drugs/medication
- primary health care team relationships
- NHS structure
- assessment (particularly when working to a time limit)
- knowledge of mental health referral pathways and procedures
- brief focused therapy methods.

Input is also recommended on interactive processes within families, systemic theory and audit and evaluation methodologies.

The Sainsbury Centre for Mental Health, in its document *The Capable Practitioner* (2001a), extends the concept of competence to capability – which is the ability to *apply* the necessary knowledge, skills and attitudes to a range of complex and changing settings. The capability framework combines the notions of the effective practitioner with that of the reflective practitioner, identifying five areas are for continuing development. These are:

1. Ethical practice.
2. Knowledge of mental health and mental health services, including policy and legislation.
3. Process of care, including effective communication and partnership with users and carers, assessment, care-planning and coordination.
4. Interventions: medical and physical, psychological, social and practical.
5. Applications to specific settings: primary care, community based care, continuing care.

The Sainsbury Centre and the Department of Health have completed a mapping exercise of training and education in mental health across a whole range of regions, disciplines, institutions and academic levels. Standards of training and education have been mapped against minimum criteria, in line with the recommendations of many policy initiatives, including the *National Service Framework for Mental Health* (Department of Health, 1999a) (see, for example, Musselwhite, Maclean & Walsh, 2004.) Such documentation provides an extensive list of training that is available and practitioners would be well advised to examine the report most relevant to their region or area.

7.5   Should I seek extra (and specialist) supervision when working with clients who have a history of mental illness?

Much has been done over recent years to address the issue of standardisation in regard to the provision of counselling supervision. Yet its implementation varies across contexts, geographical regions and disciplines, particularly in NHS mental health practice. In 2001 Freeth wrote: 'As a doctor and psychiatrist I am used to dealing with the frustration of working in an environment that is not particularly alert to the supervisory and support needs of staff' (2001, p. 223). Etherington (2001, p. 260) adds that 'where supervision does occur in the medical world it is more often concerned with "case management" than with reflexive practice, therapeutic aspects of the work or the worker's emotional responses to patients – although there are now a few exceptions'.

Although many experienced and skilled supervisors may feel that their understanding of the supervisory relationship is transferable across different settings, as a user of these supervisory services it is important to ascertain that a supervisor has at least some knowledge of the setting within which the counsellor works. A supervisor cannot and does not need to know everything, of course; however, it is perhaps particularly important for a supervisor to become acquainted with the necessary and relevant knowledge pertaining to working with a specialist mental health client group.

This might include knowledge and understanding of:

- Classifications of mental illness.
- Mental health assessment and referral pathways to and from the counsellor.
- The needs of both a primary care practice and of a counsellor working in such a setting, and the potential conflicting nature of these.
- The use of pharmaceutical drugs and the possible implications for counselling.
- Practical issues, such as note keeping in an NHS setting, audit and evaluation, appointment system, management of caseload and other administrative measures.
- The difficulties and demands of working with a high turnover of clients, who are mostly short term.
- NHS organisational structures, primary health care team relationships, hierarchies and possible 'power' struggles.
- Ethical and legal issues regarding, e.g. accountability – who is clinically responsible?
- Working within a team and the impact on confidentiality.

Working with clients who have a history of mental illness can be very demanding, provoking in counsellors at times concerns over their own 'sanity' and boundaries. Counsellors who have also been 'users' of mental health services may have an increased capacity to empathise with and validate the experiences of clients (and perhaps unconsciously, rather than through disclosure, provide hope); but they may also be more at risk of 'psychic infection' or vicarious traumatisation, which can undermine their sense of self in terms of security and identity.

A trusting supervisory relationship with someone who understands the continuum of mental health (and who has faced their own 'madness') can provide a safe space to name thoughts and fears and to understand rather than be overwhelmed by the experience.

Although most counselling training has modules on mental health and psychopathology, these are sometimes limited. Working with issues of mental health brings many difficulties and requires specialist knowledge. It may be difficult to find suitable courses to boost knowledge (see Question 7.4). Good professional supervision can, over an extended period, help to fill that gap through information, education and the sharing of experience.

In addition, the time-limited nature of most mental health work results in a quick turnover of clients with the ensuing difficulty of and emotional responses to many and frequent endings. (For a more detailed discussion of the difficulties around ending and the part played by supervision see Question 6.7.)

Working with clients with a history of mental illness brings the counsellor into close contact with other professionals involved in that individual's care plan,

and working collaboratively can bring difficulties and new challenges to people
who are used to working independently. A supervisor with specialist experience
will be better placed to understand the potential boundary and role conflicts
that can arise. One area of concern may be confidentiality (see also Question
6.4), which can be explored fully in supervision. There may be other practical issues such as shared space, time boundaries, misunderstandings of role
and so on. A supervisor who has had experience of the reality of the context is
better placed to facilitate an exploration of anything that is troubling the
counsellor with regard to the practical and ethical aspects of working in a team.

One of the possibilities of working with people with severe mental difficulties is that in the involvement of numerous carers, 'splitting' may occur:
supervision permits an exploration of this phenomenon. A counsellor's
desire for self-esteem may seduce her into accepting the positive at face
value, without considering the possibility of whether the client is splitting
between one therapist who is 'good' and another who is 'bad'.

Having said all this, there may be difficulty in finding a supervisor with
the relevant knowledge and experience; one possibility is to seek specialist
supervision as and when necessary. Networking and peer supervision can
provide another form of support, allowing ideas, experiences, skills and
knowledge to be shared, and providing a safe space to explore both feelings
and the limitations of what can and cannot be achieved.

7.6   What are the sections of the Mental Health Act that are of particular relevance to counsellors and psychotherapists?

The Mental Health Act of 1983 is based on the findings of a Royal Commission
set up in the 1950s, and on legislation in 1958 and 1959; thus it is over 45
years since mental health legislation was last fundamentally reviewed. The 1983
act is very complex, written in inaccessible language, covering many different
areas, including compulsory admission to hospital, consent to treatment and
the right to appeal. There is also a separately published Code of Practice, which
is regularly reviewed, and the Act itself is in the process of being updated.

As it currently stands the parts of the Mental Health Act that seem to be of
particular relevance to counsellors include the following sections.

Section 1 – concerning definitions

This section attempts to provide a legal rather than a medical definition
of the types of problems that might be covered under the Mental Health Act.
It begins by defining 'mental disorder', which is described as mental illness,

arrested or incomplete development of the mind, psychopathic disorder and any other disorder or disability of the mind. Specifically named are severe mental impairment, mental impairment, psychopathic disorder and mental illness. This last category highlights the circular and unsatisfactory nature of these definitions. In this latter category of mental illness the Act states clearly only what it is not: that is, that people must not be said to have a mental illness by reason only of promiscuity or other immoral conduct, sexual deviancy or dependence on alcohol or drugs.

This statement, intended as a safeguard against inappropriate detention, does not seem to appear in the same way in the new bill (which is under review as I write), about which there are many concerns. The existing law does not exclude treatment of those with a dual diagnosis, but it does make sure that mental health service users do not have their needs confused with those whose problems arise from a different source such as drug or alcohol abuse or criminal behaviour. One of the main concerns over the current draft Mental Health Bill is around definition, which is now much broader. Mental disorder is now defined as: 'Any disability or disorder of the mind or brain, which results in impairment, or disturbance of mental functioning'. Human rights campaigners are concerned that the new legislation is as vague as the 1983 Act, but could now include those suffering from epilepsy, or learning difficulties, and, for example, the elderly.

Alongside the broader definition, the current bill contains a broader set of criteria for compulsory treatment. This is another major area of contention: its opposers see this as giving clinical staff the right to impose treatment on people who do in fact have the capacity to decide for themselves.

As noted in Chapter 2, mental illness covers a vast spectrum of experience and there is a distinction between much mental illness and those disorders labelled as 'severe personality disorders'. Whilst there is no doubt about the need to protect the public where there are potential, actual or perceived dangers, O'Brien (2003), in a poorly attended House of Commons debate, commented: 'We must take care to recognise that some mental illness is defined in terms of the potential risk to self, as opposed to a risk or even danger to the public at large'. It is argued that the draft bill focuses on danger rather than on what is treatable. O'Brien continued: 'If we look at mental health from the point of view of what is treatable, we can, as part of our responsibility as a civilised society, examine what can make the life and participation in society of certain individuals better, rather than examining the danger to, and protection of, those of us lucky enough not to be afflicted.'

Section 2 – concerning admission to hospital for assessment

This section provides information regarding the authority needed for someone to be detained in hospital for assessment for up to 28 days and is based on two medical recommendations. This application is usually made when someone is compulsorily admitted to hospital for the first time.

Section 3 – concerning admission to hospital for treatment

If a person is well known to the psychiatric service and little formal assessment is needed, an application for them to be admitted under Section 3 may be made. Again two medical recommendations are necessary and the initial duration is six months, with the possibility of renewal for a further six months, and then for a year at a time.

In the proposed bill the making of a treatment order – the third stage – is contained in clauses 28–50. A major criticism here is that there are no clear criteria for care plans, and that social and cultural differences appear to be overlooked although they are relevant to care plans. There is a call for the inclusion of a professional from a social work or other professional background (and this could include counsellors and psychotherapists) to provide broader expertise within the tribunal. As it stands the tribunal both authorises detention and challenges it.

Section 4 – emergency admission

This section covers emergency admission for up to 72 hours initially; the police may be involved, or in the case of voluntary patients in hospital doctors have 'holding powers' of up to 72 hours. Nurses have similar powers for up to six hours. For further discussion of the implications of the sections referring to hospital admission see Question 7.7.

Critics of the bill highlight the need for objective evidence of mental disorder, according to human rights law, as there is a perceived danger that stereotyped assumptions about certain groups will cause difficulties. (See Chapter 4 for issues concerning ethnic minorities, those with learning disabilities, women, young offenders and the elderly.)

Section 117 – aftercare arrangements

This section gives the statutory authorities (District Health Authorities) a duty to make arrangements for a person's continuing support and aftercare. To this end the Care Programme Approach (CPA) was introduced in 1991. This attempts to provide the basis for the care of people with mental health needs once discharged from hospital. In many cases the care plan begins before discharge and recognises the links with social services departments. It is as part of this aftercare planning that counsellors and psychotherapists can make an important contribution, helping the individual to integrate back into society, as well as providing support and care for the carers. Primary care once again becomes the point of interface, and for many it becomes the only point of contact with mental health services.

Whereas the 1983 Act gives rights to a patient discharged from compulsory powers to the services that he or she needs, until they are no longer required, there is no reference to this in the current draft bill. Whilst the tribunal has an overview of the provision of aftercare it has no power to rectify or enforce any shortfall of the services offered.

The new bill appears, therefore, to many to be a retrograde step, returning to the days of the asylum, rather than continuing the move towards care in the community. The benefits of community care have been somewhat obscured by the 'panic' engendered by media reporting of isolated incidents of violence committed by the 'mentally ill'. Whereas the horror of these cases on an individual basis must never be underestimated, statistics show that violence is more closely linked to substance or alcohol abuse, social class, the male gender and youth than to mental illness (see Freshwater (2003) for a comprehensive debate on these matters).

Overview of the current debate

In September 2003, the British newspaper *The Sun* published a headline 'Bonkers Bruno locked up', the implication being that he was 'mad', 'bad' and 'dangerous'. After many complaints the headline was changed and the Sun launched an appeal in Frank Bruno's name to raise funds for SANE, asking Marjorie Wallace (chief executive of SANE) to write for the paper on the subject of mental illness:

> The truth is that Frank Bruno was ill and taken to a hospital – not a 'mental home' – in much the same way as if he had had a heart attack or had been injured in a road accident. The difference is that if someone is having a mental breakdown they may become so ill that they no longer realise how ill they have become, resist help and may have to be sectioned under the Mental Health Act.

The Sun is not alone. In 1996 a survey reported that 75 per cent of tabloid editorials about mental health linked mental distress to violence; and, on BBC1 and ITV 70 per cent of news items featuring mental distress also linked this to violence (Adlam, 1990). Understanding is changing, but slowly: in 1985 when *The Times* ran a campaign, the 'Forgotten Illness', names were changed and shadowy pictures were used. In July 2002, The *Independent on Sunday*, as part of its mental health campaign, ran a six-week appeal for SANE where celebrities spoke about their own experiences, being happy to be named and photographed.

In 2001 a successful exhibition, '1 in 4', of photographs of prominent people who have had mental health problems was shown initially at The Oxo Tower in London. Public attitudes it seems are changing but perhaps it took the breakdown of a folk hero to make the tabloid press realise the alienation of their readers, caused by demeaning words that 'are like verbal tattoos stigmatising not only mentally ill people but further isolating their families' (Wallace 2003).

However, it was following the public outcry at the murder of Lin Russell and her daughter Megan by Michael Stone in 1998 that the government first announced plans to detain those with severe mental disorders who have not committed a crime. Stone had a severe personality disorder that was 'untreatable' and so could not be detained under the Mental Health Act.

Following a committee appointed in 1998, a Green Paper on the *Reform of the Mental Health Act* was published in November 1999. This was followed by a White Paper in December 2000, and a Draft Mental Health Bill in 2002, with an accompanying consultation document in June of that year. It was severely criticised by over 60 organisations (The Mental Health Alliance), including the British Psychological Society, the Royal College of Psychiatrists and the charity Mind, for extending the powers of compulsory treatment, and for its focus on public safety rather than the care and treatment of those deemed 'mentally ill'. Since then the Bill has failed to feature in at least two of the Queen's speeches.

Many fear that the draft bill reinforces the misperception that people with mental health problems are dangerous. Gostin (2002) suggests that the reforms are based on (at least) two false assumptions: namely that violence is closely associated with mental illness 'which is not true. In fact, data suggests that as a population people with mental disabilities are not disproportionately dangerous'. He also questions whether dangerousness can be predicted, claiming that past violence and drug or alcohol abuse are the best predictors, whereas there is little or no evidence to suggest that psychiatric assessment or prognosis can predict future violence.

Mental health legislation and criminal justice legislation seem to have become conflated and this response is perhaps driven more by the call for 'law and order' than by any desire to improve care for the mentally ill. Of course the government has a responsibility to protect the public from dangerous people, but the approach is arguably too heavy handed and driven by scare not care. The inevitable consequences will be instilling more fear in the public and increasing the stigma attached to mental ill health, as well as decreasing the likelihood of someone seeking help and sharing any dangerous thoughts. Counsellors know the importance of a safe space to explore these darker thoughts as an alternative to 'acting out' in the family or wider community.

In September 2002 Mind commissioned a poll concerning the proposed changes to the Mental Health Act. The pollsters, NOP, found high levels of concern over doctors' powers to force patients with mental health problems to take medication. Thirty-seven per cent said they would be deterred from asking their GP for help in dealing with depression, a figure that rose to 52 per cent of the 15–24 age group, who are particularly at risk from depression. If this is the case for those with depression then the fear of compulsory detention is likely to deter people with significant personality disorders or other mental health problems from seeking help. This does not really safeguard the public either and possibly even increases the risk.

Carvel (2002) quotes one poster from the campaign against the new reform: 'Locked up for no offence. Force-fed drugs. Labelled mad. Would you seek treatment? One in four of us will experience mental health problems – the new mental health bill will only make things worse.' As counsellors and psychotherapists working in private practice or within the NHS and other services it is important to remain vigilant as to the difficulties facing those who have a mental health problem and where appropriate add our voices to the debate. There is clearly public concern over safety, and the 1983 Act has its loopholes, but many see the new reform as over-inclusive and ill defined. Certainly this is the public's perception, but because these concerns are not 'headline grabbing' there is a danger that they will go unheeded.

It also seems that the proposed mental health legislation is in some ways contrary to the *National Service Framework for Mental Health* (see Chapter 1), which sets seven national standards for mental health services, with the aim of improving the quality of and reducing variations in services to patients and service users. It is intended to include round-the-clock crisis teams for emergencies, more mental health beds and improved training for general practitioners. The NSF appears to emphasise community and in-patient services, caring for and empowering, whereas the Mental Health Act emphasises compulsory treatment or detention in hospital. Thus the focus falls on severe mental illness rather than on primary care for mental health – the area where most counsellors are involved. To neglect the full range of treatment available to, and required by, the majority of those who suffer from mental illness raises some ethical and professional questions for counsellors. O'Brien (2003) states: 'There is a real concern that, partly because of targets, there is too little flexibility to recognise the huge value that counselling and psychotherapy can add to the provision of mental health services.' Counsellors and psychotherapists in the United Kingdom, whether or not they are mindful of it, will be affected by the Mental Health Act (1983) and any new mental health legislation. Those with a political and active interest and a keen eye to health policy are no doubt already aware of the impact of health reform on both the provision of services (particularly the marginalised practitioners such as counsellors) and of course those providing the services for marginalised groups like the mentally ill.

7.7   One of my clients has broken the law and I have been asked to act as a character witness, commenting specifically on her mental state. Should I take legal advice?

The short answer to this is an emphatic 'Yes' – but, of course, it is not that simple. As a counsellor or psychotherapist, whether working privately or for the NHS, professional indemnity insurance is a must, and most insurance providers have a free legal help-line for advice on issues such as this. In addition, the practitioner should consider contacting the professional body of which they are a member, as this question highlights a potential ethical minefield, calling as it does for a complicated juggling of the six ethical principles: *justice, fidelity, autonomy, beneficence, non-maleficence* and *self-respect*.

Fidelity is about being trustworthy and honouring the trust placed in the counsellor by the client. Trust is the cornerstone of confidentiality and any statement as a character witness, invited to comment on the client's mental state, will involve breaking this confidentiality. The *Ethical Framework for Good Practice* (British Association for Counselling and Psychotherapy, 2002) clearly states that any disclosure of information about clients should be restricted to 'furthering the purposes for which it was clearly disclosed' (2002, p. 3). Few people undertake counselling or psychotherapy for the purpose of having evidence provided in court of their character.

The principle of *autonomy*, however, enshrines respect for the client's right to be self-governing; so it is advisable to enquire whether this request to appear as a character witness has come from the client's solicitor or from the prosecution. The Data Protection Act of 1984 gives the data subject the right of access to information held about them, and the 1998 Act states that data may only be used for the purpose for which it was originally collected. The sharing of information is based on 'informed consent', which is 'any freely given, specific and informed indication of wishes by which the data subject signifies his agreement to personal data relating to him being processed'.

Counsellors may be sent a form with the client's signature, but just to accede without first checking with the client does not fulfil the duty of care. Even if the request comes from the client's representative with the client's consent, the principle of *beneficence*, which means acting in the client's best interests, requires that before any disclosure is made the counsellor should check whether the consent given is truly 'informed consent'. It cannot be assumed that the solicitor has talked this through with the client, and in any case there is an inevitable power imbalance between someone who is alleged to have broken the law and their legal representative. It is the responsibility of the counsellor, therefore, to explain as fully as possible, and in terms that are meaningful and can be understood by the client, the nature of the disclosure, its possible consequences, and how the information will be used and stored. Does the client fully understand that any comment which is based on the counsellor's notes (which may ultimately be subpoenaed) will be typed or copied by clerks and secretaries and will eventually, at the end of any court case, become public documents? It is perhaps a good idea to get a written letter from the client stating that the implications of disclosure have been fully discussed. This signifies 'informed consent' and will protect the counsellor against claims for breaches of confidentiality.

The principle of *self-respect* means the application of all the other principles to oneself. Depending on the type of notes that are kept by the counsellor, confidentiality may be endangered. Notes that records of dreams, emotions, ideas and thoughts are little more than 'hearsay' evidence – relevant to the counselling process, but open to misinterpretation and the charge of being 'unprofessional' when viewed by others who record things in a more factual way. Much of the work is linked to the unconscious processes, which are hard to document. As Bollas (2003, p. 157) argues, can any form of notes 'even remotely be considered to represent the immaterial psychic reality of a psychoanalysis'? He encourages therapists to refuse to comply with a court order that violates the confidentiality of a patient: 'We must argue that confidentiality is held by our profession – not by our patients – so that we may discuss our patients with colleagues, clear in our minds that in so doing we are not referring our patients to the criminal justice system' (Bollas, 2003, p. 157).

Once again supervision has an important part to play in facing this issue. A supervisor would be aware of the strict procedures set out in the Data Protection Act regarding the process of accessing notes. For further information and extensive coverage of these issues see Chapter 5 on 'Record-Keeping' in the companion book on the Law (Jenkins, Keter & Stone, 2004).

References

Ader R & Cohen N (1975) Behaviourally conditioned immunosuppression. *Psychosomatic Medicine* **37**: 333–340.

Adlam D (1990) Television news and the cultivation of otherness. *Collected Original Resources in Education* **17**: 22.

Ahuja A (2003) *God on the Brain: is Religion Just a Step Away from Mental Illness?* Available from: http://www.timesonline.co.uk/article/0,,7-648955,00.html. (Accessed 20 May 2005.)

American Psychiatric Association (1994) *The Diagnostic and Statistical Manual of Mental Disorders (DSM-1V)*. Washington DC: American Psychiatric Association.

Anderson K (1994) *Mosby's Medical, Nursing and Allied Health Dictionary*, 4th edn. London: Mosby.

Anderson EM & Lambert MJ (1995) Short-term dynamically oriented psychotherapy: A review and recta-analysis. *Clinical Psychology Review* **9**: 503–514.

Angus L & McLeod J (eds.) (2004) *The Handbook of Narrative and Psychotherapy: Practice, Theory and Research*. Thousand Oaks, CA: Sage.

Armstrong E (1997) *The Primary Mental Health Care Toolkit*. London: Department of Health.

Baker R (2003) *Understanding Panic Attacks and Overcoming Fear*. Oxford: Lion.

Barnes M & Bowl R (2001) *Taking over the Asylum: Empowerment and Mental Health*. Basingstoke: Palgrave.

Basu R (2004) Mental health problems in childhood and adolescence. In Norman I & Ryrie I (eds.), *The Art and Science of Mental Health Nursing: A Textbook of Principles*. Milton Keynes: Open University Press.

Beck AT, Ward CH, Mendelson M, Mock J & Erbaugh J (1961) An inventory for measuring depression. *Archives of General Psychiatry* **4**: 53–63 (and also **38**: 764–768).

Bhaumik S, Collacott RA, Gandhi D & Duggirala C (1995) A naturalistic study in the use of antidepressants in adults with learning disabilities and affective disorders. *Human Psychopharmacology: Clinical & Experimental* **10**(4): 283–288.

Bhugra D, et al. (2000) Factors in the onset of schizophrenia: a comparison between London and Trinidad samples. *Acta Psychiatrica Scandinavica* **101**(2): 135–141.

Bhui K, McKenzie K & Gill P (2004) Delivering mental health services for a diverse society. *British Medical Journal* **329**(7462): 363–364.

Bhui K, Stansfield SA, Hull S, Priebe S, Mole F & Feder G (2003) Ethnic variations in pathways to specialist mental health care: a systematic review. *British Journal of Psychiatry* **162**: 473–480.

Bobgan M & Bobgan D (1987) Psychoheresy: The psychological seduction of Christianity. Santa Barbara, CA: Eastgate. Cited in Zinnbauer BJ & Pargament KI (2000) Working with the sacred. *Journal of Counselling and Development* **78**(2): 162–172.

Bollas C (2003) Confidentiality and professionalism in psychoanalysis. *British Journal of Psychotherapy* **20**(2): 157–176.

Bouras N, Holt G & Gravestock S (1995) Community care for people with learning disabilities: Deficits and future plans. *Psychiatric Bulletin* **19**: 134–137.

Bower P, Jerrim S & Gask L (2004) Primary care mental health workers: role expectations, conflict and ambiguity. *Health and Social Care in the Community* **12**(4): 336–345.

Boydell J, et al. (2001) Incidence of schizophrenia in ethnic minorities in London: ecological study into interactions with environment. *British Medical Journal* **323**(7325): 1336–1338.

Bracken P & Thomas P (2001) Post psychiatry: a new direction for mental health. *British Medical Journal* **322**: 724–727.

Brennan G (2004) The person with a perceptual disorder. In Norman I & Ryrie I (eds.), *The Art and Science of Mental Health Nursing: A Textbook of Principles*. Milton Keynes: Open University Press.

British Association for Counselling and Psychotherapy (2002) *Ethical Framework for Good Practice in Counselling and Pscyhotherapy*. Rugby: BACP.

British Association for Counselling and Psychotherapy (2005a) *Ethical Guidelines for Researching Counselling and Psychotherapy*. Rugby: BACP.

British Association for Counselling and Psychotherapy (2005b) Media News (last update Thursday 12th May 2005). Available from: www.bacp.co.uk. (Accessed 14 May 2005.)

Broome A (ed.) (1989) *Health Psychology: Processes and Applications*. London: Chapman and Hall.

Brown GW (1996) Life events, loss and depressive disorders. In Heller T, Reynolds J, Gomm R, Muston R & Pattison S (eds.), *Mental Health Matters*. Basingstoke: Palgrave.

Burman E, Gowrisunkur J & Walker K (2003) Sanjhe Rang/Shared colours, shared lives: a multicultural approach to mental health practice. *Journal of Social Work Practice* **17**(1): 63–76.

Burnard P (1987) Spiritual distress and the nursing response: theoretical considerations and counselling skills. *Journal of Advanced Nursing* **12**(3): 377–382.

Burr J (2002) Cultural stereotypes of women from South Asian communities: mental health care professionals' explanations for patterns of suicide and depression. *Social Science and Medicine* **55**: 835–845.

Burton M (1998) *Psychotherapy, Counselling and Primary Health Care*. Chichester: John Wiley & Sons.

Busfield J (2001) *Rethinking the Sociology of Mental Health*. Oxford: Blackwell.

Cameron M, Edmans T, Greatley A & Morris D (2003) *Community Renewal And Mental Health: Strengthening the Links*. London: Kings Fund Publications.

Carroll BJ, Feinberg M, Smouse PE, Rawson SG & Greden JF (1981) The Carroll Rating Scale for Depression I: Development, reliability, and validation. *British Journal of Psychiatry* **138**: 194–200.

Carvel J (2002) Alleged abuse of dementia patients investigated. The Guardian, 6 December 2002.

Casement P (1985) *On Learning from the Patient*. London: Routledge.

Chesler P (1996) *Women and Madness*. London: Allen Lane.

Churchill R, et al. (2001) A systematic review of controlled trials of effectiveness and cost effectiveness of brief psychological treatments for depression. *Health Technology Assessment* **5**(35): 1–6.

Craig T (2000) Severe Mental Illness: Symptoms, signs and diagnosis. In Gamble C & Brennan G (eds.), *Working with Serious Mental Illness: A Manual for Clinical Practice*. London: Balliere Tindall.

Crits-Christoph P (1992) The efficacy of brief dynamic psychotherapy: A meta-analysis. *American Journal of Psychiatry* **159**: 325–333.

Crome I, Ghodse H, Gilvarry E & McArdle P (eds.) (2004) *Young People and Substance Misuse*. London: Gaskell Publications.

Cummings N & Sayama M (1995) *Focussed Psychotherapy*. New York: Bruner.

Dallos R (1996) Psychological approaches to mental health and distress. In Heller T, Reynolds J, Gomm R, Muston R & Pattison S (1996) (eds.), *Mental Health Matters*. Basingstoke: Palgrave.

Davies S, Naik CP & Lee AS (2001) 'Depression, suicide and the NSF'. *British Medical Journal* **322**: 1500–1501.

Delor F & Hubert M (2000) Revisiting the concept of vulnerability. *Social Science & Medicine* **50**: 1557–1570.

Department of Health (1992) *The Health of the Nation*. London: DoH.

Department of Health (1993) *Services for People with Learning Disabilities and Challenging Behaviour or Mental Health Needs (The Mansell Report)*. London: HMSO.

Department of Health (1999a) *National Service Framework for Mental Health*. London: DoH.

Department of Health (1999b) *Our Healthier Nation*. London: DoH.

Department of Health (1999c) *Improving Quality in Primary Care: A Practical Guide to the NSF for Mental Health*. London: DoH.

Department of Health (2000) *The NHS Plan*. London: DoH.

Department of Health (2001) *Making it Happen*. London: DoH.

Department of Health (2001) *Mental Health Policy Implementation Guide*. London: DoH.

Department of Health (2001) *Treatment Choice in Psychological Therapies and Counselling: Evidence Based Clinical Practice Guideline*. London: DoH.

Department of Health (2002a) *Development of Mental Health Care for Women*. London: DoH.

Department of Health (2002b) *Women's Mental Health: Into the Mainstream. Strategic Development of Mental Health Care for Women*. London: DoH.

Department of Health (2003) *Attitudes to Mental Illness*. London: DoH.

Department of Health (2004) *Organising and Delivering Psychological Therapies*. London: DoH.

Depression Alliance (2003) *Treatment for Depression*. Available from: http:www.depressionalliance.org. (Accessed 20 May 2005.)

Desai S (2003) From pathology to postmodernism: a debate on 'race' and mental health. *Journal of Social Work Practice* **17**(1): 95–102.

Durkheim E (1964[1895]) *The Rules of Sociological Method*. New York: Free Press.

Egan G (1990) *The Skilled Helper*, 4th edn. California: Brooks Cole.

Ellis A (2001) An Interview with Albert Ellis. Available from: www.psychotherapy.net. (Accessed 15 May 2005.)

Etherington K (2001) *Counsellors in Health Settings*. London: Jessica Kingsley.

Fee D (ed.) (2000) *Pathology and the Postmodern*. London: Sage.

Fernando S (2002) *Mental Health, Race and Culture*, 2nd edn. Basingstoke: Palgrave.

Finlay-Jones R (1989) Anxiety. In Brown GW & Harris TO (eds.), *Life Events and Illness.* New York: Guildford Press.

Flaherty JA, Channon RA & Davis JM (1989) *Psychiatry: Diagnosis and Therapy— A LANGE Clinical Manual.* Stanford, CT: Appleton and Lange.

Frances AJ, First MB & Widiger TA (1991) An A-Z guide to DSM-IV conundrum's. *Journal of Abnormal Psychology* **100**: 407–412.

Frankl V (1984) *Man's Search for Meaning.* Boston: Beacon Press.

Franklin DJ (2003) *Psychology Information Online. Depression: Information and Treatment.* Available from: http://www.psychologyinfo.com/depression/. [Accessed 15 May 2005.]

Freeth D (2001) Sustaining inter-professional collaboration. *Journal of Inter-professional Care* **15**(1): 37–46.

Freshwater D (1998) Polarity and unity: The healing power of symptoms. *Complementary Therapies in Nursing and Midwifery* **5**(5): 136–139.

Freshwater D (2003) Researching mental health: Pathology in a postmodern world, *NT Research* **8**(3): 161–172.

Freshwater D, Walsh L & Storey L (2001) Prison health care: developing leadership through clinical supervision. *Nursing Management* **8**(8): 10–13.

Freshwater D, Walsh L & Storey L (2002) Prison health care part 2: developing leadership through clinical supervision. *Nursing Management* **8**(9): 16–20.

Freud S (1914 [1959]) *On the History of the Psycho-Analytic Movement.* Standard Edition **14**: 3–66. London: Hogarth Press.

Freud S (1926 [1959]) *Inhibitions, Symptoms and Anxiety.* Standard Edition **20**: 77–174. London: Hogarth Press.

Freud S (1930 [1961]) *Civilization and its Discontents*, trans and ed. James Strachey. New York: WWNorton.

Friedell M & Bryden C (2002) A word from two turtles: A guest editorial. Dementia: *The International Journal of Social Research and Practice* **1**(2): 131–133.

Gartner J, Larson D & Allen G (1991) Religious commitment and mental health: a review of empirical literature. *Journal of Psychological Theology* **19**: 6–25.

Gendlin E (1990) The small steps of the therapy process. In Lietaer G, Rombauts J & Van Balen R (eds.), *Client-Centred and Experiential Psychotherapy in the Nineties.* Leuven: Leuven University Press.

Gergen KJ (1991) *The Saturated Self: Dilemmas of Identity in Contemporary Life.* New York: Basic Books.

Gergen M & Gergen K (2003) *Social Construction.* London: Sage.

Glanville J & Lefebvre C (2001) Accessing the evidence on clinical effectiveness. *Effectiveness Matters* **5**(1). Available from http://www.york.ac.uk/inst/crd/pdf/em51.pdf.

Goater N, King M & Cole E (1999) Ethnicity and outcome of psychosis. *British Journal of Psychiatry* **175**: 34–42

Goldberg DP (1972) *The Detection of Psychiatric Illness by Questionnaire.* Oxford: Oxford University Press.

Goldberg D (1978) *Manual for General Health Questionnaire.* Slough: NFER.

Gomm R (1996) Mental Health and Inequality. In Heller T, Reynolds J, Gomm R, Muston R & Pattison S (eds.), *Mental Health Matters. A Reader.* Basingstoke: Palgrave.

Gostin L (2002) Favouring fright over facts. *The Guardian*, 12 September.

Greenberg B & Witzum E (1991) Problems in the treatment of religious patients. *American Journal of Psychotherapy* **45**(4): 554–565.

Grof S (1976) *The Dimensions of Dying and Rebirth: Lectures from the 1976 Easter confer-ence at the Association for Research and Enlightenment*, inc. Stanislav Grof, Hugh Lynn Cayce, Raynor C. Johnson. Virginia Beach, VA: A.R.E. Press.

Hamilton M (1967) Development of a rating scale for primary depressive illness. *British Journal of Social & Clinical Psychology* 6: 278–296.

Hammersley D & Beeley L (1992) The effect of medication on counselling. *Counselling* 3(3): 162–164.

Harper DJ (1995) Discourse Analysis and 'Mental Health'. *Journal of Mental Health* 4: 347–357.

Harris E & Barraclough B (1998) Excess mortality of mental disorder. *British Journal of Psychiatry* 173: 11–53.

Hauke C (2000) *Jung and the Post Modern. The Interpretation of Realities.* London: Routledge.

Health Which (2002) Online at http://www.which.net/media/pr/health2002.html. (Accessed 9 August 2005.)

Healy D (1993) *Psychiatric Drugs Explained.* Guildford: Mosby.

Heller T, Reynolds J, Gomm R, Muston R & Pattison S (1996) (eds.), *Mental Health Matters.* Basingstoke: Palgrave.

Helman CG (2000) *Culture, Health and Illness*, 4th edn. Oxford: Butterworth-Heinemann.

Henderson P (1996) Starting Work in General Practice: The induction of counsellors into the primary mental health care team. *Counselling and Primary Care Trust Supplement 2*, pp. 20–24. Staines: CPCT.

Henkel V, Mergl R, Kohnen R, Maier W, Möller H-J & Hegerl U (2003) Identifying depression in primary care: a comparison of different methods in a prospective cohort study. *British Medical Journal* 326: 25.

Hofstede G (2001) *Cultures Consequences: Comparing Values Behaviours Institutions and Organizations across Nations*, 2nd edn. Thousand Oaks, CA: Sage.

Hornby S & Atkins J (eds.) (2000) Collaborative Care: *Interprofessional, Interagency and Interpersonal*, 2nd edn. Oxford: Blackwell Synergy.

Horney K (1991) *Neurosis and Human Growth.* New York: Norton.

Howard KI, Moras K, Brill PL, Martinovich Z & Lutz W (1986) Evaluation of psycho-therapy: efficacy, effectiveness, and patient progress. *American Psychologist* 51: 1059–1064, cited in Feltham C (ed.) (2002) *What's the Good of Counselling and Psychotherapy?* London: Sage.

Hudson-Allez G (2003) *Assessment for Primary Care Counselling.* Seminar 5 April 2003, CPC, Cambridge.

Ion RM & Beer MD (2003) Valuing the past: The importance of an understanding of the history of psychiatry for healthcare professionals, service users and carers. *International Journal of Mental Health Nursing* 12(4): 237–242.

Jacobs M (1998) *The Presenting Past: the Core of Psychodynamic Counselling and Therapy*, 2nd edn. Buckingham: Open University Press.

Jacobs M (1999) *Psychodynamic Counselling in Action*, 2nd edn. London: Sage.

Jacobs M (2000) *Illusion: A Psychodynamic Interpretation of Thinking and Belief.* London: Whurr.

Jacoby M (1990) *Individuation and Narcissism.* London: Routledge.

Jahoda M (1958) *Current Concepts of Positive Mental Health.* New York: Basic Books.

James J & Prilleltensky I (2002) Cultural diversity and mental health: towards integrative practice. *Clinical Psychology Review* 22: 1133–1154.

Jenkins GC (2002) 'Good money after bad? The justification for the expansion of counselling services in Primary Health care.' In Feltham C (ed.), *What's the Good of Counselling and Psychotherapy?* London: Sage.

Jenkins P, Keter V & Stone J (2004) *Psychotherapy and the Law: Questions and Answers for Counsellors and Therapists.* London: Whurr.

Joint Health Surveys Unit of the National Centre for Social Research and University College, London (2000) Ethnic Minority Psychiatric Illness Rates, Department of Health Publications and Statistics. Available from: http://www.dh.gov.uk/PublicationsAndStatistics/fs/en. (Accessed 9 August 2005.)

Jones GM & Miesen BM (eds.) (1991) *Care-giving in Dementia: Research and Reflections.* London: Routledge.

Joseph P (2001) Faith or delusion? At the crossroads of religion and psychosis. *Journal of Psychiatric Practice* **7**(3): 163–172.

Jung CG (1964a) *Man and his Symbols.* London: Aldus Books.

Jung CG (1964b) *Memories, Dreams, Reflections.* London: Fontana.

Jung CG (1968) The Collected Works (CW), edited by H Read, M Fordham & G Adler, 9(1) *The Archetypes and the Collective Unconscious.* London: Routledge.

Jung CG (1987) *Dictionary of Analytical Psychology.* London: Ark Paperbacks.

Katon W, Lin E, Von Korff M, Russo J, Lipscomb P & Bush T (1991) Somatisation. A Spectrum of Severity. *The American Journal of Psychiatry* **148**(1): 34–40.

Keady J & Ashton P (2004) The older person with dementia or other mental health problems. In Norman I & Ryrie I (eds.), *The Art and Science of Mental Health Nursing: A Textbook of Principles.* Milton Keynes: Open University Press.

Keating F, Robertson D, McCulloch A & Francis A (2002) *Breaking the Circles of Fear.* London: Sainsbury Centre for Mental Health.

Kendall RE (1996) The nature of psychiatric disorders. In Heller T, Reynolds J, Gomm R, Muston R & Pattison S (eds.), *Mental Health Matters. A Reader.* Basingstoke: Palgrave.

Kendall RE (2001) Foreword: Why Stigma Matters. In Crisp AH (ed.), *Every Family in the Land: Understanding Prejudice and Discrimination against People with Mental Illness.* London: Robert Mond Memorial Trust.

King M, Sibbald B, Ward E, Bower P, Lloyd M & Gabbay M (2000) Randomised controlled trial of non-directive counselling, cognitive-behaviour therapy and usual general practitioner care in the management of depression as well as mixed anxiety and depression in primary care. *Health Technology Assessment* **4**: 19.

Kitwood T (1996) Some problematic aspects of dementia. In Heller T, Reynolds J, Gomm R, Muston R & Pattison S (eds.), *Mental Health Matters. A Reader.* Basingstoke: Palgrave.

Kleinman A (1980) *Patients and Healers in the Context of Culture: An Exploration of the Borderland Between Anthropology, Medicine and Psychiatry.* London: University of California Press.

Kleinman A (1988) *The Illness Narratives: Suffering, Healing and the Human Condition.* New York: Basic Books.

Kleinman A & Becker A (1998) Sociosomatics: the contribution of anthropology to psychosomatic medicine. *Psychosomatic Medicine* **60**(4): 389–393.

Kohut H (1977) *The Restoration of the Self.* New York: International Universities Press.

Kopp S (1991) *If You meet Buddha on the Road, Kill Him!* London: Sheldon Press.

Kopta SM, Howard KI, Lowry JL & Beutler LE (1994) Patterns of symptomatic recovery in time-unlimited psychotherapy. *Journal of Consulting and Clinical Psychology* **62**: 1009–1016.

Lambert MJ & Bergin AE (1994) The effectiveness of psychotherapy. In Bergin AE & Garfield SL (eds.), *Handbook of Psychotherapy and Behaviour Change*, 4th edn. New York: Wiley.

Lesniewicz P (2004) Women in crisis: An integral study of spiritual emergency in Christian women. *Dissertation Abstracts International* **64**(11-B): 57–66.

Leuba JH (1896) A study in the psychology of religious phenomena. *American Journal of Psychology* **7**: 309–385.

Lewis C, Sullivan C & Barraclough J (1994) *The Psychoimmunology of Cancer*. Oxford: Oxford University Press.

Lindley P, O'Halloran P & Juriansz D (2001) *The Capable Practitioner: A Framework and List of the Practitioner Capabilities Required to Implement The National Service Framework for Mental Health*. London: Sainsbury Centre for Mental Health.

Littlewood R & Lipsedge M (1982) *Aliens and Alienists–Ethnic Minorities and Psychiatry*. Harmondsworth: Penguin.

Lockhart RA (1983) *Words as Eggs: Psyche in Language and Clinic*. Dallas: Spring Publications.

Ludwig M (1999) *Gene Research and Body Psychotherapy*. Available from: http://www.eabp.org/gene_research.htm. (Accessed 15 May 2005.)

Lukoff D (1985) Diagnosis of mystical experiences with psychotic features. *Journal of Transpersonal Psychology* **17**(2): 151–181.

Lukoff D (1998) From spiritual emergency to spiritual problem: The transpersonal roots of the new DSMIV category. *Journal of Humanistic Psychology* **38**(2): 21–50.

Manning N (2001) Psychiatric diagnosis under conditions of uncertainty: personality disorder, science and professional legitimacy. In Busfield J (ed.), *Rethinking the Sociology of Mental Health*. Oxford: Blackwell Publishing.

Mansell JL (1993) *Services for People with Learning Disabilities, Challenging Behaviour or Mental Health Needs, Project Group Report*. London: HMSO.

Martin P (1997) *The Sickening Mind*. London: Flamingo.

Masters REL & Houston J (1966) *The Varieties of Psychedelic Experience*. New York: Holt, Rinehart and Winston.

Matthews D (1995) Challenging Service. *Nursing Times* **91**(23): 59.

Mellor-Clarke J (2000) *Counselling in Primary Care in the Context of the NHS Quality Agenda: The Facts. Psychological Therapies Research Centre*. University of Leeds, Rugby: BACP.

Meltzer H, Gill B, Petticrew M & Hinds K (1995) *Physical Complaints, Service Use and the Treatment of Adults with Psychiatric Disorders, OPCS Surveys of Psychiatric Morbidity in Great Britain, report 1*. London: HMSO.

Mental Health Foundation (2000) *Strategies for Living: Report of a User Led Research into People's Strategies for Living with Mental Distress*. London: Mental Health Foundation.

Mental Health Foundation (2003) *Black Spaces Project*. London: MHF.

Mirowsky J (1989) *Social Causes of Psychological Distress*. New York: Adline de Gruyter.

Moore T (1992) *Care of the Soul*. New York: Harper and Collins.

Moore T (1996) *Re-enchantment of Everyday Life*. New York: Harper Collins.

Morgan C, Mallett R, Hutchinson G & Leff J (2004) Negative pathways to psychiatric care and ethnicity: the bridge between social science and psychiatry. *Social Science and Medicine* **48**: 739–752.

Munro A (1999) *Delusional Disorder. Paranoia and Related Illnesses.* Cambridge: Cambridge University Press.

Murray CJL & Lopez AD (1997) Global mortality, disability and the contribution of risk factors: Global Burden of Disease Study. *Lancet*, **349**: 1436–1442.

Musselwhite CBA, Maclean L & Walsh L (2004a) *Mental Health Awareness for Prison Staff: A Case Study at HMP High Down.* Presented at the Sharing Good Practice in Prison Health Conference, Royal York Hotel, York, UK, 25–26 May.

Musselwhite C, Freshwater D, Schneider K & Galvin K (2004b) *Mapping of Education and Training for Mental Health Practitioners in the South West.* Bournemouth: IHCS, Bournemouth University.

Nathan MM (2001) Overcoming barriers to spiritual care. *Sacred Space* **2**(4): 18–24.

National Institute for Mental Health in England (2003) *Inside Outside: Improving Mental Health Services for Black and Ethnic Minority Communities in England.* London: Department of Health.

National Institute for Mental Health in England (2004) *Promoting Mental Health: A Resource for Spiritual and Pastoral Care.* London: DoH.

National Institute for Mental Health in England (2005) www.ementalhealth.com. (Accessed 20th May 2005.)

NHS Centre for Reviews and Dissemination (1998) *Effective Healthcare Bulletin: Deliberate Self-harm* **4**(6). York: University of York.

Nino AG (1997) Assessment of spiritual quests in clinical practice. *International Journal of Psychotherapy* **2**(2): 193–211.

NSW Genetics Education Program (2003) Available from: http://www.genetics.com. au. (Accessed 20 May 2005.)

O'Brien S (2003) Member for Eddisbury (Mr O'Brien). House of Commons Hansard Debate: 14 Oct 2003 : Column 28WH.

Palmer D (2001) Identifying delusional discourse: issues of rationality, reality and power. In Busfield J (ed.), *Rethinking the Sociology of Mental Health.* Oxford: Blackwell Publishing.

Parry G (1996) Using research to change practice. In Heller T, Reynolds J, Gomm R, Muston R & Pattison S (eds.), *Mental Health Matters. A Reader.* Basingstoke: Palgrave.

Parry G (1997) *Psychotherapy Services in England: Review of Strategic Policy.* London: Department of Health, NHS Executive.

Parry G (1999) Brief versus open-ended counselling in primary care. *European Journal of Psychotherapy, Counselling and Health* **2**(1): 7–18.

Paykel ES, et al. (1997) The Defeat Depression Campaign: psychiatry in the public arena. *American Journal of Psychiatry* **154** (Festschrift suppl): 59–65.

Pearce N, Foliaki S, Sporle A & Cunningham C (2004) Genetics, race, ethnicity, and health. *British Medical Journal* **328**: 1070–1072.

Perkins R & Repper J (2004) Rehabilitation and recovery. In Norman I & Ryrie I (eds.), *The Art and Science of Mental Health Nursing: A Textbook of Principles.* Buckingham: Open University Press.

Persinger MA (1999) *Neuropsychological Bases of God Beliefs.* New York: Praeger.

Pieper JZT (2004) Religious coping in highly religious psychiatric inpatients. *Mental Health, Religion and Culture* **7**(4): 349–363.

Raleigh VS (1996) Suicide patterns and trends in people of Indian subcontinent and Caribbean origin in England and Wales. *Ethnicity and Health* **1**(1): 55–63.

Ramachandran VS & Hubbard EM (2001) Synaesthesia – a window into perception, thought and language. *Journal of Consciousness Studies* **8**: 3–34.

Ramachandran VS & Hubbard EM (2003) Hearing colors, testing shapes. *Scientific American* **288**(5): 42–49.

Rampes H (2004) Complementary and alternative therapies. In Norman I & Ryrie I (eds.), *The Art and Science of Mental Health Nursing: A Textbook of Principles*. Buckingham: Open University Press.

Reading B & Jacobs M (eds.) (2002) *Addiction: Questions and Answers for Counsellors and Therapists*. London: Whurr.

Rogers CR (1951 [Reprinted in 2002]) *Client Centred Therapy: Its Current Practice, Implications and Theory*. London: Constable.

Rogers CR (1975) A theory of personality and behaviour. In Brown H & Stevens R (eds.), *Social Behaviour and Experience*. London: Hodder and Stoughton.

Rose D, Ford R, Lindley P, Gawith L & the KCW Mental Health Monitoring Users' Group (1998) In *Our Experience: User-Focused Monitoring of Mental Health Services*. London: Sainsbury Centre for Mental Health.

Rosenhan DL (2001) On being sane in insane places. *Science*, **179**: 250–258.

Rowan, J (2002) *The transpersonal psychotherapy and counselling*. London: Routledge.

Royal College of Psychiatrists (1998) *Changing Minds*. London: Royal College of Psychiatry.

Royal College of Psychiatrists (2002) *Mental health and growing up. Serious Mental Illness*. Fact sheet, 2nd edn. Available from: http://www.rcpsych.ac.uk/info/mhgu/. (Accessed 20 May 2005.)

Ryrie I & Norman I (2004) *The Art and Science of Mental Health Nursing*. Buckingham: Open University Press.

Sacks O (1985) *The Man who Mistook his Wife for a Hat*. New York: Touchstone.

Sainsbury Centre for Mental Health (1998) Getting Ready for User Focused Monitoring (UFM), A Guide for Mental Health Service Providers, Users and Purchasers. *In User Empowerment – Further Information*. Mind Factsheet. Available from: http://www.mind.org.uk/Information/Factsheets.

Sainsbury Centre for Mental Health (2001a) *The Capable Practitioner*. London: Sainsbury Centre for Mental Health.

Sainsbury Centre for Mental Health (2001b) *A General Practitioner's Guide to Managing Mental Illness*. London: Sainsbury Centre for Mental Health.

Samuels A, Shorter B & Plaut P (1986) *A Critical Dictionary of Jungian Analysis*. London: Routledge.

SANE (2003) Factsheets: *Schizophrenia the Forgotten Illness, Medical Methods of Treatment, Psychological Methods of Treatment, Alcohol, Drugs and Mental Illness*. Available from: http://www.sane.org.uk/public_html/About_SANE/sane_publications.shtm. (Accessed 20 May 2005.)

Saunders SM (2000) Examining the relationship between the therapeutic bond and the phases of treatment outcome. *Psychotherapy* **30**: 206–218.

Saunders SM (2002) The clinical effectiveness of psychotherapy. In Feltham C (ed.), *What's the Good of Counselling and Psychotherapy?* London: Sage.

Shaffer D, Gould MS & Fisher P (1996) Psychiatric diagnosis in child and adolescent suicide. *Archives of General Psychiatry* **53**: 339–348.

Shorter E (1994) Medical Sociology – From the mind into the body: The cultural origins of psychosomatic symptoms. Cited in Horwitz AV, *Contemporary Sociology*, **23**(6): 891.

Simpson S, Corney R, Fitzgerald P & Beecham J (2000) A randomised controlled trial to evaluate effectiveness and cost-effectiveness of counselling patients with chronic depression. *Healthcare Technology Assessment* **14**: 36.

Singleton N, Bumpstead R, O'Brien M, Lee A & Meltzer H (2001) *Psychiatric Morbidity Among Adults Living in Private Households*. London: The Stationery Office.

Sloan T (1996) *Damaged Life: The Crisis of the Modern Psyche*. London: Routledge.

Starbuck ED (1899) *The Psychology of Religion. An Empirical Study of the Growth of Religious Consciousness*. New York: Charles Scribners Sons.

Stimpson GV (1999) *Dual Diagnosis: The Co-morbidity of Psychotic Mental Illness and Substance Misuse*. Executive summary of editorial board (63). London: Centre for Research on Drugs and Health Behaviour, Imperial College.

Stone M (1993) Long term outcome in personality disorders. *British Journal of Psychiatry* **162**: 200–213.

Svartberg M & Stiles TC (1991) Comparative effects of short-term psycho-dynamic psychotherapy: a meta-analysis. *Journal of Consulting Clinical Psychology* **59**: 704–714.

Svartberg M & Stiles TC (1993) Efficacy of brief dynamic psychotherapy (letter). *American Journal of Psychiatry* **150**: 684.

Tepper L, Rogers SA, Coleman EM & Newton Maloney H (2001) The prevalence of religious coping among persons with persistent mental illness. *Psychiatric Services* **52**: 660–665.

Townsend P, Whitehead M & Davidson N (eds.) (1992) *Inequalities in Health: the Black Report and the Health Divide*, 2nd edn. London: Penguin.

Tudor K (1996) Mental health promotion at work. In Trent DR & Reed CA (eds.), *Promotion of Mental Health*. Vol 5. Aldershot: Avebury.

Tudor K (2004) Mental health promotion. In Norman I & Ryrie I (eds.), *The Art and Science of Mental Health Nursing*. Buckingham: Open University Press.

Turner R (1995) Religious or spiritual problem. A cultural sensitive diagnostic category in the DSM IV. *Journal of Nervous and Mental Disease* **183**(7): 435–444.

Van der Moolen C (2002) Doctor, please make me well again! On clients having severe subjective health complaints (the Somatoform Disorder). In Watson JC, Goldman RN & Warner MS (eds.), *Client-Centred and Experiential Psychotherapy in the 21st Century*. Ross-on-Wye: PCCS Books.

Walker M (2003) *Abuse: Questions and Answers for Counsellors and Therapists*. London: Whurr Publishers.

Walker M & Jacobs M (2004) *Supervision: Questions and Answers for Counsellors and Therapists*. London: Whurr Publishers.

Wallace M (2003) I forgive you my sun. *The Sun*, 4 December 2003.

Warner S (1996) Special women, special places: Women and high-security mental hospitals. In Burman E, Aitken G, Alldred P, Allwood R, Billington T, Goldberg B, Gordo-Lopez AJ, Heenan C, Marks D & Warner S (eds.), *Psychology Discourse Practice: From Regulation to Resistance*. London: Taylor & Francis.

Watson K (1994) Spiritual emergency: Concepts and implications for Psychotherapy. *Journal of Humanistic Psychology* **34**(2): 22–45.

White M (2004) Folk psychology and narrative practices. In Angus LE & McLeod J (eds.), *The Handbook of Narrative and Psychotherapy*. London: Sage.

Wilbur, K (2000) *A theory of everything*. Shambhala: Boston.

Williams J (1999) Social inequalities and mental health. In Newes C, Holmes G & Dunn C (eds), *This is Madness: A Critical Look at Psychiatry and the Future of Mental Health Services*. Ross-on-Wye: PCCS Books.

Williams JW Jr, Noel PH, Cordes JA, Ramirez G, Pignone M (2002) Is this patient clinically depressed? *Journal of the American Medical Association* **287**: 1160–1170.

Wilson M & Francis J (1997) *Raised Voices – African-Caribbean and African Users Views and Experiences of Mental Health Services in England and Wales*. London: Mind.

World Health Organization (1992) *The ICD-10 Classification of Mental and Behavioural Disorders*. Geneva: World Health Organization.

World Health Organization (WHO) Collaborating Centre for Mental Health Research UK (2000) *WHO Guide to Mental Health in Primary Care*. London: Royal Society of Medicine Press.

Yalom I (1999) *Loves Executioner and Other Tales of Psychotherapy*. New York: Harper Perennial.

Yen J & Wilbraham L (2003) Discourses of culture and illness in South African mental health care and indigenous power, part 1: Western psychiatric power. *Transcultural Psychiatry* **40**(4): 542–561.

Zinnbauer BJ & Pargament KI (2000) Working with the sacred. *Journal of Counselling and Development* **78**(2): 162–172.

Zung WW (1965) A Self-rating Depression Scale. *Archives of General Psychiatry* **12**: 63–70.

Index

pain 48, 49
panic 44
personality disorders 3–4, 47, 52, 64,
    110, 111
personality types 47–8
phantom limb pain 49
physical symptoms, mental health and *see*
    psyche–soma relation
policy development *see* mental health
    policy
political construction of mental
    illness 55–7
    see also social model
power relations 55–7, 62
prevalence of mental illness 7
primary care
    confidentiality 86–8
    depression screening 28, 29
    evidence based counselling 93–8
    hospital discharge planning 108–9
    liaison teams 9
    Mental Health Act reforms 110–11
    mental health policy 9–10, 81
    mental health workers 81–3
    private practice counsellors 84
    psychosocial interventions 100–2
    referrals 84–6, 89
    time limited counselling 89–92, 94, 100
    trainee counsellors 89
    training courses 102–3
    treatment choice 98, 99–100
    voluntary counsellors 88
    waiting list prioritisation 88
private practice 83–4, 89–92, 100, 102–4
professional indemnity insurance 112
professional issues
    character witnesses 112–13
    evidence based practice 93–8
    psychosocial interventions 100–2
    supervision 103, 104–6, 113
    training courses 100–4
    treatment choice 98–100
    see also collaborative working
psyche–soma relation 39–54
    anxiety 43, 44–5, 46, 47, 48
    attending to bodily symptoms 42–3, 46
    cancer 49–50
    cardiovascular conditions 46, 47
    collaborative working 84

complexity 39
conflicting messages about 40
cultural factors 42, 52, 58
depression 43, 44, 46, 47, 48–9, 51, 54
development of psychotherapy 41–2
gastrointestinal disorders 46
hallucinations 49
immune system 47–8
incidence of co-morbidity 39–40
inherent meaning of disease 41
loss of bodily functions 39
medical disorder with psychological
    symptoms 46
medical model of illness 5, 40
neurological disorders 46
personality factors 47–8
problems with dualistic
    approach 42–3
pulmonary disorders 46
self-harm 51–3
separate vs linked accounts 40–3
socioeconomic conditions 43
stress 43, 44–5, 47
substance misuse 53–4
terminally ill clients 50–1
psychodynamic models 5, 6
psychodynamic work 93–8
psychological models 4–7
    see also behavioural models; medical
        model; social model
psychoneuroimmunology 48
psychoses 3, 4, 51, 52, 53, 54, 58–9
    see also bipolar disorder; psychotic
        clients; schizophrenia
psychosocial interventions 100–2
psychotic clients
    Alzheimer's disease 67–8
    religious delusions 75–7
    spiritual emergencies 80
    substance misuse 54
    tendency to spiritual themes 77–9
    value of psychotherapy 32–3
    see also bipolar disorder; schizophrenia
public attitudes 109–10
pulmonary disorders 46
purpose, spirituality and 73

'race', culture and 57–8, 63
racism 60–1, 62–3